Understanding Independent School Parents

The Teacher's Guide to Successful Family-School Relationships

Understanding Independent School Parents

The Teacher's Guide to Successful Family-School Relationships

By Michael G. Thompson, Ph.D. and Alison Fox Mazzola, M.Ed.

To the members of the So-Called Healthy Group. You enrich and support my life.

~ *Michael G. Thompson*

To my husband, whose urging brought this book to life.

~ *Alison Fox Mazzola*

Contents

Part One:
Understanding Independent School Parents
By Michael G. Thompson Ph.D.

Chapter One

Chapter Two

Chapter Three

Chapter Four

Part Two:
What Teachers Can Do
By Alison Fox Mazzola, M.Ed.

Chapter Five

Chapter Six

Introduction, 2011

In the six years since Alison Fox Mazzola and I first published our teachers' guide to successful family-school relationships under the flag of the National Association of Independent Schools, the relationship between independent school parents and their children's teachers has only grown more intense. Tuitions have risen, college admissions are increasingly selective, high-stakes testing has proliferated in the public sector and fears of bullying – especially internet bullying – continue to grow. From our perspectives as a psychologist and a classroom teacher, we have seen parents become ever more worried about their children's education. They wonder constantly about what their role should be in their children's learning.

Most parents, of course, are grateful when their children (mostly) love school; most recognize the positive impact that teachers make on their children's lives. However, a small minority chooses to act as their children's advocates, agents, coaches, co-teachers, and sometimes apologists. They see themselves as responsible for homework completion, curricular standards, for playing time on teams and for the outcome of their child's friendships and social interactions.

College-educated mothers are spending almost twice as much time with their children per week than they did 20 years ago, research tells us. This display of love and attention is not without its downside. In my fellow school psychologist and author Rob Evans' witty turn of phrase, many parents are no longer, "preparing the child for the path." Instead, they are "preparing the path for the child."

The debate about the role of parents in their children's school lives crescendoed – loudly – in 2011 with the publication of Amy Chua's book, *The Battle Hymn of the Tiger Mother*, and the release of the movie *Race to Nowhere*. Professor Chua threw down the parenting gauntlet, challenging American moms and dads to embrace higher standards for their children's educations, in the manner of Chinese mothers. She insisted that truly responsible parents do not allow their children to take a part in school plays or go to summer camps. No, they require their children to get only A's, they send them to summer school to improve their grades, they call them "fat" rather than "overweight," they require them to play only piano or string instruments, and to study, study, study.

Chua's characterization of herself as a "Tiger Mom" galvanized parents and teachers. Knowing of our interest in the parent-teacher relationship, parents began to introduce themselves to Alison and me with a defensive phrase, insisting, "I'm not a Tiger Mom," conceding "I'm kind of a Tiger Mom," and sometimes, "I'm a Tiger Mom." Teachers began to use the phrase as well, replacing the clichéd and dismissive term "helicopter mom" with this novel and even scarier sobriquet. Meanwhile, *Race to Nowhere* suggested that independent school parents, with their relentless academic ambitions, and independent schools with their endless homework demands, were driving their children to suicide.

What's a parent – or a teacher – to do in the face of such conflicting messages from the culture? These debates ratcheted up the intensity level between parents and schools, teachers and parents. Schools began to cultivate the parent-school relationship, extolling the virtues of community and rewriting their handbooks to offer parents a more defined role in school life. There was much talk of the "parent-school partnership," but it was rarely defined in detail. Meanwhile, upon the advice of consultants, some independent schools began revising their re-enrollment contracts so that they could decline to invite back students whose parents did not have a trusting or civil relationship with the school. In other words, independent schools began to reserve the right to expel parents who behave badly.

The upshot of all this is that parents have become a bigger part of school life than they were when Alison and I began our respective careers as a teacher and a school psychologist. It also means that school administrators and teachers are spending more time focused on the demands and concerns of parents than they ever did in the past. "Parent management" has become a bigger part of all teachers' jobs because administrators expect them to communicate with parents more effectively.

What has not changed is the fundamental quest at the heart of the parent-teacher relationship: a search for trust between adults who love their children and other adults who want to help those children reach their full educational potential.

Understanding Independent School Parents

We believe that the current intense examination of the parental role in schooling requires both parties to understand each other better. That is why we are re-publishing our teacher's guide to understanding independent school parents. Our target audience is teachers, because parents do not have the same motivation to understand teachers that teachers do to understand them. We do not expect them to buy this book, hence our one-sided title. However, we don't believe parents will be put off if they do read this guide. We're not giving away state secrets here. Our approach to parent-teacher relationships is based on two simple ideas: that it is sometimes scary for parents to turn their children over to teachers whom they only get to know through their children, and it is sometimes unnerving for teachers to have highly educated, tuition-paying parents looking over their shoulders when they are trying to do an effective, creative, and compassionate job in the classroom.

Although Alison and I have some war stories to tell about the relationship between parents and teachers, we believe our understanding of the parent-teacher relationship is based on deep empathy for both parties, for one simple reason: both of us are parents and both of us have been teachers.

Alison believes that parents are genuinely disoriented by the vast distance between the pedagogical practices that went on in classrooms when they were children and the present approach to teaching and learning, particularly in constructivist schools. The more hands-on, inquiry-focused approach of today's more sophisticated teachers can be uncomfortable for parents because the learning process doesn't involve the vocabulary quizzes and math sets that they remember from their own childhoods. We are all reassured when things look the way we remember them, even if what we remember was incredibly boring, and even if brain science and educational research have long since demonstrated that there are better ways to teach.

In recent years, I have written about good parents – thoughtful, well-meaning people – who are trapped in four mental traps that I call paradoxes: the paradox of control; the paradox of choice; the paradox of information; and the paradox of "the great parent."

Contemporary parents have had unprecedented levels of control over their children's lives from birth, or even from before birth if you consider ultrasound technology and pre-natal surgery. That control continues with the radio receiver in the nursery to the online homework site, from a password-protected portal on the school's website to follow daily grades to personalized videos from summer sports camps to help a child improve in baseball. The paradox is that the more control parents have over their children, the less they trust their children to be competent and independent. All these ways of managing kids' lives make it tougher and tougher for parents to let their children go.

The same thing has happened with information. Parents have come to believe that the more they know about their children's school journey, the better it will be.

That's simply wrong. I regularly ask adults to tell me what percentage of their tenth grade day at school their mothers knew about. Did their moms know 5 percent, 10 percent, or 50 percent of the details about their academic, social and extracurricular lives? Most adults report that their moms knew less than 10 percent about what went on in their day; many say they worked hard to keep it that way. Yet they now believe that if they have more information about their child's school day *they* will be able to better guide their child to success. Is that true? When I watch a second grader and her mom battle for two hours over 20 minutes of homework I wonder how much the parent is helping the child to love school.

Today's parents seem to want more opportunities and choices for their children. They believe that choice will make their children happier. Barry Schwartz, in his wonderful little book, *The Paradox of Choice: Why Less is More*, has demonstrated conclusively that in most situations, a huge increase in choices leads to lower rates of happiness. Yet parents continue to fight for choice, as if getting admitted to six colleges will really help a senior feel better about himself or herself than getting positive letters from three colleges would. You can only go to one college and the job of finding a great fit can be derailed by those extra admissions letters.

Finally, it can be a great burden to a child to have a mother or father need to be "a great parent." If your mom or dad is intensely focused on your every achievement, if they are keeping every gold star from kindergarten and every sticker from first grade in laminated pages in a notebook, it raises the stakes dizzyingly high. If you do badly in school you not only fail in your own right, you destroy your parent's self-esteem, as well. Yes, high expectations can be motivating for children; research has proven that. But unrelenting parental investment in a child's academic performance is likely to make him or her anxious, constricted and unwilling to take risks.

Teachers have three great gifts that they can give every parent. First, they can so enjoy teaching their subject that they inspire a child to want to learn. Second, they can describe a child's school journey in some detail (but not every day!). Third, they can put a child's struggles into a developmental context, such as, "Most sixth-grade girls worry a lot about friendship," or "Most seventh-grade boys are still pretty disorganized." What a relief for parents to know that no matter how much information they have and control they think they want, human development remains in charge.

Even with these gifts in their hands, it can be tricky for teachers to talk to high-power independent school parents. That is why Alison and I wrote a guide specifically designed for independent school teachers. We think that, in spite of the current intense focus on the "cultivation" of children, as Malcolm Gladwell describes it, the fundamental realities of parenting have not changed and that if teachers can better understand the psychological dilemmas of parents they can provide them with reassurance and wisdom. In turn, their children will relax a bit and will take advantage of the extraordinary opportunities for learning, growth and joy that are to be found in independent schools.

Michael G. Thompson, Ph.D.
Arlington, Massachusetts

Introduction, 2004

This book is the creative resolution of one teacher's frustrated search for a guide to help her deal with challenging independent school parents. In her early years of teaching, Alison Fox Mazzola felt that she had encountered more than her share of difficult parents and unsupportive administrators. Some parents were unable to communicate effectively enough to work as part of a team for the education of their children. One family in particular — a relentlessly anxious and intimidating couple — almost drove her out of the profession. Because she loved children and schools and had an abiding interest in curriculum, she was angry that one set of out-of-control parents had come so close to ending her teaching career. Distressed that she had to bear parental attacks alone, and frustrated at the lack of a straightforward primer about how to think about and work with challenging parents, she soldiered on, developing strategies on her own.

The closest thing Alison found to the guidebook she yearned for was a daylong workshop, "Understanding Families and Dealing with Difficult Parents," that I conduct on an annual basis at David Mallery's Westtown Teachers' Seminar in Pennsylvania. She had traveled to the seminar from California looking for the spiritual refreshment and intellectual revitalization that teachers have found there for 41 years. She had been intrigued by the title of my presentation; at least *someone* was using the words "difficult parents." What she did not anticipate was that during the workshop she would find herself at the center of a cathartic role-play, portraying the very parent who had tormented her endlessly over some undelivered playground equipment. She was also surprised that all the other teachers in the room empathized and identified with her as they laughed and shared their own tales of scary moms and intimidating dads. It was clear at Westtown that every teacher had a story or stories about what I call "exotic" parents. Alison realized that the teachers in that one room, for their own survival, had developed a wealth of effective techniques for working with challenging families.

It still concerned Alison that there was no book on the subject. She thought about writing it herself but felt she lacked the overview of independent schools that such a guide required. Then, two years after her Westtown summer, an opportunity appeared. I visited her school in California to conduct a faculty workshop. She requested 15 minutes of my time, reminded me of our Westtown meeting and her memorable role play (I remembered it), and presented me with a five-page proposal for this book.

"We should write a guide for teachers to help them with difficult parents," she announced. I was taken aback, I admit. I'd never had a stranger tell me what book I ought to write, nor had I ever had someone propose herself out of the blue as my co-author. Furthermore, I had just finished writing *The Pressured Child* (Ballantine, 2004) and had promised myself and my family that I would not write another book for two years.

But Alison's logic was compelling. Too many teachers struggle alone, and often ashamed, while trying to manage difficult parents — and I have seen their pain as I travel around the country working with faculties.

When Alison approached me, I had spoken with numerous teachers who had experienced miserable years, left their schools because of unsupportive administrators, or even left the profession, at least temporarily, because of a few destructive parents. I had been conducting faculty workshops about dealing with difficult parents for a decade. I knew that independent schools in general, as well as schools of education, do an inadequate job of preparing teachers for the parent body with whom they are going to interact. But I had never felt that I had the material to write a book on the subject. So I said to Alison, "But I don't have the detailed case material to write such a book." She proceeded cheerfully to produce stacks of files. "I've been documenting," she said. "I have the notes from my own experiences."

And that's the story of how we — two relative strangers, in a conversation lasting less than half an hour — came to write this book together. We approached Nancy Raley in the publications office at the National Association of Independent Schools; she enthusiastically embraced the idea, and here we are.

One of the facts of life in independent schools is that parents, by virtue of paying tuition, are customers. That is a reality that underlies all the school talk of "community" and "partnership." What does it require of a teacher when a parent is a customer? Certainly parents are paying for good teaching and dedicated care for their children. But what does a teacher owe the customer-parent beyond that? A teacher cannot, like the owner of the local dry cleaner, say to a complaining parent, "If you don't like the job we do, take your business elsewhere." That would mean yanking a child out of school, which is almost always unacceptable. For the sake of the children we must struggle to understand what is making some parents so unhappy and we must assume all of us — teachers, administrators, and parents — are devoted to the best interests of the child.

Independent schools are service organizations. All of us involved in independent schools serve the needs of parents and children, and we recognize that parents are legitimately entitled to some level of attention from an organization to which they pay tuition. Attention? Of course. But how much is too much? What does "service" translate into as a practical matter? Does it mean that a teacher should rush to the airport with a homework assignment because a child is leaving on a trip and forgot it? Does it mean a teacher should be available by phone or e-mail at any hour of the day or night? Does it mean a teacher has to tolerate being besieged by phone calls and e-mails complaining that a serious injustice is being done because the new playground equipment hasn't arrived? What if the phone calls keep coming, along with twice-daily e-mails and occasional personal attacks? What happens then?

This book aims to answer those questions. One important note: although the case studies in this book were inspired by real situations we have made every effort possible to disguise details that might reveal the individuals involved. We have switched the ages, grades, and genders of some children involved and we have sometimes conflated two or three stories into one. In some places we have frankly fictionalized elements of the stories to deepen the disguise. None of the e-mails we quote, for example, use the actual words of the parents who wrote them — though the spirit of the originals remains. We do this to protect the parents, the schools, and most important, the children, involved.

Our intention in this book is not to ridicule parents. We understand that every parent, no matter how challenging his or her behavior may be for school personnel, starts from a place of love for a child. Every parent, no matter how illogical he or she may appear to a teacher or psychologist, is fighting for "the best" for his or her child. As parents ourselves, we identify with and respect the core motivations in every parent. But for the purposes of this book, we want to help prepare teachers for the unexpected requests and unwelcome attacks that can suddenly manifest themselves in a parental phone call or a casual conversation at back-to-school night.

To preserve the authenticity of our two points of view, we decided to retain the "I" voice for our separate sections of the book. The descriptions of Alison's conferences with her most challenging parents require the immediacy of her emotional "I" responses. My years as a classroom teacher were brief, and my overview of the relationship between parents and schools comes from my perspective as a psychologist, a trained family therapist, and, most important, a parent. As the father of two independent school students I have endured some humiliating meetings on the parental side of things and that perspective can only be expressed in first person.

We hope you will find this book useful and that it will make your work in independent schools more successful and more fun. Our mission is to help teachers better enjoy their complex and important jobs — and stay in the profession. Sometimes that requires teachers to move outside their comfort zone and directly question the assumptions and behavior of parents. We know we cannot make it possible for you to please every parent, but with these ideas we believe we can help even your challenging parent-teacher relationships go more smoothly. We think this will mean that you will have some more energy for the young people in your classroom. After all that's why you became a teacher in the first place.

Alison and I know that in independent schools, every teacher, sooner or later, will be confronted with a difficult, even irrational, parent. They are out there; they are part of the landscape of our schools. It may not happen every year, but it will happen. We hope this book helps you prepare for that eventuality, live through it, and come out smiling.

Michael G. Thompson, Ph.D.
Arlington, Massachusetts

Part One:
Understanding Independent School Parents

By Michael G. Thompson, Ph.D.

Chapter One

Teachers and Parents: An Uneasy Relationship

In my work in schools, I have noticed that many teachers find contact with families one of the most vexing and perplexing aspects of their work. The most gifted teacher, with a profound understanding of children, can feel baffled and inadequate when faced with a demanding or unrealistic family. Why should that be? And why do advisors sometimes dread family conferences? Why do administrators choose to deal only with a child when a partnership with the family might improve the situation? Why do so many teachers, all of them with vast experience in human relations — in their classrooms and with their own families — shy away from becoming involved with families in a professional context?

There are a number of reasons. First, and most important, teachers do not choose teaching as a profession because they want to work with adults; they choose teaching because they love the time they spend with children. Many teachers I know experience themselves as more effective with kids than they are with adults.

Second, most teachers are not trained to work with parents. Though many take courses in graduate schools of education, most receive no specific, academic instruction in working with families and there is precious little orientation about family dynamics when they arrive at their schools. As a result, many teachers do not feel they have the tools to manage the situations that they will be required to face. No one likes to be asked to do something for which they were not prepared.

Third, almost any teacher who has worked in an independent school has dealt with a scary parent at least once. When a teacher has been frightened by a difficult parent, he or she may remain wary of families for years afterwards. A high school teacher once described dealing with a verbally abusive father who had attacked his professionalism. He summed up the case by saying, "And now, every time a parent comes through my classroom door, I wonder, 'Could this parent be one of those?'" Lacking the training and perhaps the support to better meet the painful situation, a teacher may simply avoid it.

This is unfortunate. Fear interferes with a teacher's enjoyment of the job; it corrodes the joy he or she originally found in teaching. And because teachers are increasingly being called on to enter into a partnership with parents, avoidance is no longer an option.

According to writer Sara Lawrence-Lightfoot, the dialogue between teachers and parents is "the essential conversation." It is certainly the case that parents in independent schools, for mostly good reasons, want to develop a collaborative relationship with teachers. They also view independent schools as service organizations, which can confuse teachers. Teachers think they are in schools to teach the students, not the parents. To the teacher it is absolutely evident that those are two different constituencies with entirely different claims.

Parents do not necessarily see the distinction between service to them and good teaching for their children. For them it's all part of the same package. I was talking to an independent school parent, a high-powered business executive, and I asked him why he sent his children to an independent school. His answer was direct. "If I call the school, I want to know that someone is going to be responsive to me." I was taken aback. I had expected him to say, "It is such a fine academic institution," or "My children love it so much." Instead, he referred to *his* relationship with the institution — and in a matter-of-fact way that a teacher might well experience as aggressive or entitled. The truth of the matter was that this father was a widower raising two children and he was hungry for contact with teachers as a source of advice and information about his children. However, that is not the way it sounded to my educator's ear, and I suspect that it might not sound either benign or friendly to a teacher.

The Nature of Independent School Parents

In general, I am disposed to like independent school parents. (Indeed, I am one. Both my daughter and son attend independent schools.) I like these parents because they are committed to education; that is where they are spending their money. They don't just talk the talk; they walk the walk. A lot of wealthy people in the world do not necessarily spend their disposable income on education. Instead, they move to an affluent suburb, trust the schools whether they are trustworthy or not and use their money to buy fancy cars or boats. Not so independent school parents. A few may own boats, but all of them pay high tuitions on behalf of their children; for a majority of independent school families that's a significant sacrifice.

Who are these people who are willing to pay for their children's schooling, also while paying property taxes that support the local public schools? Of course they tend to be affluent. NAIS research tells us that to send your child to an independent day school without scholarship assistance, you need to be in the top 10 percent of incomes in the United States. To send your child to a boarding school, you need to be in the top 5 percent of U.S. incomes. Some of the better-endowed schools can offer an enormous amount of help to families. The headmaster of one long-established boarding school told me that 41 percent of his families receive some financial aid. That's wonderful, but it's also the exception to the general rule. Independent schools tend to be tuition-driven and you have to be pretty well off to send your child to one.

In general, independent school parents share these additional characteristics: They are well educated themselves; they have high expectations for what education will do for their children; they are accustomed to unusually high levels of control over their lives; and they are, on average, pretty anxious. The first two observations are empirically verifiable. The "modal" independent school couple (if you learned your statistics and recall the "mode") is a two-professional couple: a lawyer father and a physician mother. We have more of these double professional couples in independent school than any other type. These are people who have spent a lot of their lives studying; their professional careers would not exist without prolonged educational preparation. And here's the rub — they expect education to be the route to the good life for their children. In my experience, they are not interested in alternatives to college and graduate school for their offspring.

Highly educated people not only care about education and value it for their children, but they also often are frightened of or ignorant about the alternatives. That fear can make them act desperately when they think their children are not getting a quality education. It makes them want to hold schools and teachers accountable. From a teacher's point of view, the parent body at an independent school contains a lot of potential critics.

My belief in the last two characteristics I mentioned — high need for control and high anxiety — arises from my own clinical observations of the parents I have dealt with in schools. It also comes from watching my fellow parents at soccer games and school meetings. Independent school parents are not, in general relaxed, fatalistic and willing to go with the flow. They are "control freaks" and they become extremely uncomfortable when they do not have their hands on the tiller. This is a problem, of course, when it comes to childrearing. Never being fully in control is perhaps the defining feature of parenting once your children are able to walk — and it doesn't ever get better. Your sense of control is ever more unsure as they grow older.

Parents choose independent schools in part to extend their control and see their dreams for their children realized. They get upset when they see the plan start to go off the rails. Perhaps these characteristics were best expressed to me by a mother from a fine school in Ohio who, with great good cheer, declared "We're all nuts!"

Making Your Peace with Independent School Parents

The single most important thing that a teacher can do to prepare philosophically for working in an independent school is to come to terms with the nature of the parents. They are who they are. I believe it is a mistake to work in an independent school and to nurture a chronic dislike for parents while enjoying and teaching their children. Actually, it is more than a mistake; it is morally untenable. It seems to me that there is some moral disconnection if a teacher loves the school's mission, its small class size, its highly motivated students, its well-stocked labs and the trips to Europe during spring vacation all the while disliking the parents. It is, after all, the parents who influence their children's behavior, who require them to do the quantities of homework that teachers assign, and who write the checks that pay for the lab equipment and the airfares. The children, the parents and the excellent teaching environment are inextricably linked.

Teachers and Parents: An Uneasy Relationship

If you are thinking of working in an independent school, it is essential to decide that you can live with the driven, controlling and anxious people your prospective students' parents can be. It will help to remember that a huge problem in American education is disengaged parents. A third of U.S. parents tell researchers that it does not matter to them what grades their children get. Psychologist Robert Evans writes in his book *Family Matters: How Schools Can Cope with the Crisis in Childrearing* (Jossey Bass, 2004) that American parents are not sending their children to school prepared to learn. These children are not well enough focused, disciplined and nurtured to bear the demands of school. While his observations are valid, I don't think Evans is describing the majority of independent school students. The vast majority of independent school parents do prepare their children for school; as educators we need to be grateful to them for that. They make our work easier by the way they motivate their children. It may not be the worst thing in the world if the price for working in an independent school is rubbing shoulders with and listening to the complaints of over-engaged, highly educated, affluent parents.

I do recognize that some people cannot tolerate being around the entitlement and overweening expectations of some independent school parents. When teachers tell me that they really dislike the upper-middle-class assumptions that dominate their school culture, I advise them to think about teaching in another setting. There are so many children who need great teachers! If you cannot make your peace with the nature of independent school parents, and their values make you angry or envious, it will inevitably color your teaching. You cannot really embrace children when you dislike the families they come from. If you find that you are constantly railing about the privilege and the unrealistic demands of parents — things that are real — it might be a sign that you do not like the population that independent schools serve. There are understandable and totally rational reasons why you might not want to serve this particular population. Irrational fears, however, are often part of the equation.

Facing Your Fear of Parents

Some independent school parents are, by virtue of their wealth and power, a bit scary. While I think everyone can understand why teachers might quail at the power of movie moguls in West Los Angeles or be intimidated by the politician parents in Washington DC, even in the coziest community schools some latent, hidden fears can infect the relationship between parents and teachers. There are fears on both sides, but some teachers find that difficult to believe. It feels like all the power and money is on the parent side and all the vulnerability is on the teacher side.

Teachers often tell me, in all sincerity, that because parents "pay the tuition" or "are the customers" or that because the head has to fund raise from the parent body, the administration is fundamentally compromised and cannot protect teachers from parental criticisms. As one teacher told me, "Teachers can never be sure that the

Teachers and Parents: An Uneasy Relationship

administration will back them in disputes with parents, so you are always afraid."

When teachers are frightened they may speak of parents as if they are *all* potentially dangerous, as if they all are the same. When teachers say, "All parents do such-and-such," or "You know how parents are..." they are engaging in sweeping generalizations. When I hear people of common sense speak of parents in that way, I know we have entered the land of the irrational and the unexamined.

If teachers wish to be free from fear of parents, the most important thing they can do is to make a shift in their thinking. Teachers have to stop thinking about parents as if they are a monolithic block of people who are all alike, or who are all equally problematic. In my experience, the vast majority of independent school parents are reasonable and — if you will permit me this word — domesticatible, no matter how wild they may be in the short term. Without a doubt, parents are capable of becoming distressed about their children. I certainly have. That impulse is the result of the protective, mother-grizzly-bear impulse that exists in all parents. We leap to protect our children from perceived harm, often before we think the issues through. However, with good will and common sense most parents, no matter how upset they initially are about an issue, can be brought to reason. That is what the head of my daughter's school did for me when, after a casual and hurtful remark by her second grade teacher, I became furious and wrote him a six-page, single-spaced letter one night. My wife laughed at me the next morning when she spotted the letter on the kitchen counter; the head of school most diplomatically "talked me down" within a day. The teacher never knew how irate I had been.

The 5 vs. the 95 Percenters

I call parents who can be brought into a working alliance with educators the "95 Percenters." This is not because I think they actually constitute 95 percent of parents; I have not done proper empirical research on this subject. Rather I want to suggest that rational parents are the overwhelming majority and educators need to separate them from the small percentage of chronically unreasonable parents I call the "5 Percenters."

Five Percenters are parents who insist on having a negative relationship with their children's school. For a complex set of reasons they simply cannot trust the institution or the teachers in it. They will find fault with one thing after another as long as their children are in the school. Why can't they trust the school to do its job? Some are disturbed; some have terrible marriages; others drink too much or are depressed and anxious. A tiny minority of parents has character disorders that make them chronically suspicious or even outright paranoid.

A number of parents had terrible school experiences when they were children and are determined not to let the same thing happen to their kids. In psychology, we would say that such parents are in the grip of "transferential" feelings, unconscious reactions based on their own past that have no relevance to present circumstances. When parents are in the grip of irrational beliefs, such thoughts drive all their motivations. With a nice turn of phrase Catherine Steiner-Adair described such parents to me 20 years ago when she was part of the counseling staff at Phillips Andover Academy (Massachusetts). She said, "There are some parents who just want *engagement* for their *enragement*."

Finally, a few memorable parents are so fabulously narcissistic that they cannot ever get past the feeling that everything is about them. Their child's flawed performance and the school's imagined failures of empathy are seen as an attack on them and they respond accordingly.

Are there more than five percent of such parents in independent schools? If you are a veteran teacher, all you have to do is count up the number of exotic and difficult parents you have managed in the past five years and divide them by the total number of parents you have had in your classrooms and you can derive your own homegrown statistic. There is nothing scientific or sacred about these particular numbers. Once, working with a faculty at a school in New York City, I suggested that 95 percent of parents are reasonable. A teacher raised her hand and said, "This is New York. The percentages here are 80 percent reasonable, 20 percent unreasonable." Everyone laughed — and I did, as well.

I don't care where you draw the line, as long as you do draw a line between the two groups of parents and think about them as requiring a different approach. I don't

11

care whether it's 95 and 5 percent, 87 and 13, 91 and 9. Every once in a while a veteran teacher, usually a lovely person, comes up to me and says, "Oh, Dr. Thompson, this school is such a lovely place that here the percentages are really 99 and 1. People here are so nice. There are only a few very difficult parents."

I accept such amendments to my scheme graciously but I believe that the teacher in question is actually telling me more about her skill in working with parents, as well as her generosity of spirit, than she is about her school. I have never seen a school that did not have a small but steady supply of exotic parents. Some teachers are highly skilled in managing them; others are not so skilled. They are afraid, and more parents register as "difficult" for them. I encourage teachers to draw the line wherever they feel comfortable. That's the first step.

Once you have broken your parents down into two groups, the manageable majority and the chronically difficult minority, you are on the road to psychological freedom. Why? Teachers are trained to deal only with the manageable majority, the 95 percent; they should not be asked to do more than that. Using common sense and goodwill, along with a few techniques that we will teach you in this book, you should be able to develop strong, rewarding alliances with the 95 Percenters you encounter. With the rest, the untamed 5 Percenters, your job is to identify them, red flag them, and ask for help from the administration.

Teachers and Parents: An Uneasy Relationship

The Role of Administrators

Most of the administrators I have met in independent schools were once classroom teachers, and good ones at that. It is mythology that only mediocre or dissatisfied teachers move into administration. Some of the most gifted teachers I've ever known reached a point where they wanted another challenge, or wanted to influence the direction of the school, or — and here is the unexpected part — they decided they really wanted to work with adults. They underwent a fundamental shift, a life change, at the end of which teaching children was not quite as interesting to them as addressing the problems of adults had grown to be.

Administrators typically spend almost all their time working with adults, and much of it involves oiling the squeakiest wheels, both on the faculty and in the parent body. Over the years I have done an informal survey of administrators and they report that meetings and phone calls with difficult parents can occupy from as little as 10 to as much as 50 percent of their time. "And some weeks it is 90 percent," one head of school told me.

Paradoxically, teachers often fail to appreciate that administrators *want* to be doing the work they have chosen to do. Even though their school leaders come into work early every morning and appear to feel wonderful about their jobs, teachers often try to protect them from the most destructive parents. It is my contention that exactly the opposite should be the case: It is the job of administrators to protect teachers from the most difficult parents. But they cannot do so unless

13

the teachers ask for help. So once you identify a parent as a 5 Percenter, ask for help from your administration and begin to develop strategies for managing that chronically unhappy mom or dad. It's not easy — but it can be done.

Chapter Two

A Matter of Style: Understanding Family Differences

Tolstoy may have claimed that happy families are all alike, but we psychologists know that each family is different. Because they are such complex social systems, families do not easily invite comparison or understanding. To a greater or lesser extent, they are closed to the outside world. There is much that we do not know about families other than our own and we may have a hard time visualizing or conceptualizing how another family works. When that family contains one of our students, the mystery can deepen.

Some years ago I was talking to a teacher about a high school girl who was developing anorexia nervosa. As is typical with anorexics, the girl had lost a lot of weight without the parents noticing. The teacher said to me, "I don't know how this could have happened. In my family, we all had dinner together every night. My parents saw everything we ate." The teacher had difficulty imagining a family that did not sit down to dinner together most nights of the week. The truth is that there are many families — healthy families — who don't have dinner together. But this teacher just could not picture such a family.

Faced with great differences between our families and other people's families, we often fall into judgment, disbelief, simple incomprehension, or mockery. We all do it. "Look at them!" "Can you believe what they do?" "Aren't they weird?

As Jane Austen, an acute observer of families wrote in her novel, *Emma*: "For what do we live, but to make sport for our neighbors, and laugh at them in our turn?"

I want to offer teachers a way of thinking about families that will allow them to step back from judgment and take a step forward to better understand and enjoy families different from their own. Every teacher should know more about families because what children experience in their homes determines how they relate to other children, to adults, to academics, and to schools. You cannot understand a child's school difficulties without understanding the child's family and his or her place in it. Once again, Jane Austen got it right when she wrote, "Nobody who has not been in the interior of a family can say what the difficulties of an individual of that family may be."

The family is the single most powerful influence on a child's life. It is a total institution in which the child is raised, and it cuts off the child from the outside world as completely as a convent or a prison. A family has its own rules and rhythms and rights and wrongs. Children do see examples of things being done differently than their family does them. But their love and loyalty to their family makes the idea of doing things differently — at least the important things — inconceivable. As children we all believe that the way our family operated was the right way. The discovery that our family's ways might have been strange comes along in adolescence and later life. Children embrace their family's style as their fundamental reality. And they attempt to remain loyal to their family style when they come to school and are confronted with a variety of ways of being and behaving.

Psychologist and teacher Jean Piaget wrote that when a teacher stands up in front of a class of 30 children and says something, it is heard in 30 different ways. Piaget was referring to differences in the cognitive developmental level of students but his observation is equally valid with respect to a child's experience of a teacher and the tone and tempo of a classroom. Every teacher is taking 30 different children, or however many there are in the room, and trying to mold them into a family-like unit called a class. The trouble a teacher experiences in that task has everything to do with a stylistic clash between his or her own ways of doing things and the habits of the families of the children in the class. One family is very tight and disciplined; the parents and the child from that family find the classroom a bit loose, a bit too open. Another family is relaxed and laid-back; they find the classroom a little too uptight and rigidly structured.

Family Styles

In an early research study on functioning, normal families, therapists David Kantor and William Lehr found that all families differ on six dimensions: the use of time; the use of space; the characteristic energy which the family displays; how and by whom power is exercised; the predominant affect of the family; and the family's sense of meaning (what I prefer to call "identity.") If you think about these dimensions it becomes obvious that some families care about being on time and keeping a very neat house while others don't care much about punctuality and the children's toys are everywhere. Some families chug along steadily with a sustained energy; others fluctuate through periods of calm punctuated by periods of wild activity. Some families are happy-go-lucky, at least as much as life will allow. Other families define themselves in very serious terms.

It turns out that these obvious differences are evidence of three underlying "pure" types of families, according to the data Kantor and Lehr collected. Families tend to conform to a "closed" type, an "open" type or a "random" type. Of course, these are statistical findings; there are no actual pure type families. In the real world, all families are a mixture of all three. But the research found that families do have predictable styles and values.

"Closed" families have a tight boundary around them that separates them from the outside world. You don't just drop in on a closed family. These families exercise power in a top-down way, with the father customarily the "boss." They value preparation, unity, sincerity, and clarity. Open families, by contrast, have a less formidable barrier around them and tend to value tolerance, authenticity, latitude, and responsiveness. Random families are dramatically different from closed and open families. Their use of time and space are likely to be dispersed, irregular and fluctuating. They value ambiguity and whimsicality; above all they want to protect the originality and creativity of their children.

As you read about these three styles, have different families you have known come to mind? You might have pictured certain families from your school or some from movies. "The Sound of Music," for example is about a "random" character, Maria, who is kicked out of a convent because she's never on time for Mass. She finds herself in a "closed" family headed by a former naval officer, Captain von Trapp. Over time, and with love, she gradually creates an "open" family where there is more latitude and, of course, harmony. Many family sitcoms on television portray families of a certain style. The original Bill Cosby Show was the idealized image of an open family where tolerance and resolution always carried the day. If you think about it, many families in theatre and art portray one of the pure family types, such as the creative, chaotic collection of relatives in Kaufman and Hart's "You Can't Take It With You," a random family if ever there was one.

I have found that Kantor and Lehr's study helps me identify the underlying values and preferred style of functioning of the various families I encounter in my school consultation work. For example, a parent from a "closed" family might feel threatened by a progressive school, thinking it undisciplined and lacking in clarity. The parents in such a family might demand that the teacher assign more homework. I once consulted to a progressive school that had no doors on the classrooms; each one was open to a common workspace. Every year a couple of families, ignoring the architect's intentional design of the building, would offer to buy doors — "closed" boundaries — for the classrooms, as if the school had somehow forgotten them or could not afford them. A "random" family is likely to find a traditional school where students wear uniforms to be oppressive and see the uniform itself as antithetical to the whimsical spirit of their child.

Teachers, too, bring the lens of their family style to bear on schools. One visiting artist to the all-boys' school where I consult portrayed the school, in her final work of art, as creating identical round, gray balls out of colorful lumps of papier-mâché. A boys' school that emphasizes discipline and preparation struck her as antithetical to creativity. I suspect she came from a random family; many artists do.

Every teacher had a family, and therefore has a characteristic style. Every teacher, like every child, grew up intimately acquainted with the values and assumptions of his or her family of origin. As much as we try to stray from our families, as much as we try to reinvent ourselves, we have been profoundly influenced by our parents and the setting of our family. The old axiom proclaims: "The apple never falls far from the tree." When we are young many of us resent the implications of that piece of wisdom. It suggests that we could not grow up to be different from, nor avoid the failings of, the families in which we grew up. Some of us, this author included, tried to fling ourselves as far from the tree as we possibly could. In middle age, we are both humiliated and bemused to find that we're still pretty close to the roots and trunk of the tree from which we were originally launched.

Our particular styles, the way we exercise power, the tempo and rhythm and neatness (or lack thereof) of our classrooms, are always a testament to our family backgrounds. We, and the little worlds we create in our classrooms, are always part of a family style that still seems "right" to us because it is the one we know so well. It is always a shock when a child experiences our classroom, our use of power, or our tempo differently from the way we do or from the way we have imagined they would.

I was once asked to consult on the case of a third-grade girl who found her dramatic, big-voiced, expansive, and funny teacher to be quite scary. "That's impossible," declared the teacher with her voice rising in indignation. "I'm not scary!" She certainly did not scare me, because I come from a highly dramatic family. Indeed, I found her energizing and delightful. But to a shy girl and her shy mother, that teacher was terrifying.

If you are going to work successfully with parents, you have to acknowledge and accept that there are many different ways to be a family and that different families will produce a wide variety of children. Some of them will take to your style and some will not. It's as simple as that. Do children need to encounter and adapt to teachers who have different styles than their families? Of course they do. But you cannot expect that they will do so without some discomfort and friction. The first discovery on your journey to wisdom about families is to accept that the families that produce the children you teach are strikingly different from each other, and some are very different from your own. You are unconsciously as attached to your reflexive family style as they are stuck with theirs. You may want a neat, orderly classroom, but a child from a random family will find it unnecessarily structured and "fussy" in comparison to the flexible use of space at home. Irritation, misunderstanding, and outright conflict are inevitable when children from many different families gather under the metaphorical roof of their third grade teacher.

Family Politics

The second step to wisdom about children and families is to realize that students always bring their families with them to school, through their perceptions and behavior. We deal with our students' families by proxy whether we want to or not.

When they are in the classroom, children are also likely to recreate, or try to recreate, the roles they play at home. Kantor and Lehr described four recognizable "psycho-political" roles in a family, which they termed mover, opposer, follower, and bystander. These roles have nothing to do with being mother or father, older sister or younger brother. They have to do with the interaction of different personalities with one another over time and how they habitually play off against one another. In one family the father might be the "mover," in another he might be a bystander. The family's mover takes the initiative and is always coming up with ideas for games and trips. The family opposer digs in, resists the idea, finds problems with it and is often passionately, but negatively, connected to the mover. The follower represents the family's swing vote. If the mother is the follower, she sometimes supports her mover husband but at other times throws her backing behind her opposer daughter. The bystander is the most loosely connected to the family. He or she does not, for the most part, participate in the family's heated battles. That leaves the bystander with energy for friends outside the family — activities that most family members may not like or understand. However, because he or she rarely cares about family decisions, when a bystander does feels strongly about an issue he or she is likely to have a lot of influence.

What does this all have to do with the classroom? Common sense tells us a mover is going to try to recreate that role in the classroom, as will an opposer. The two are likely to meet and become antagonistic. Teachers tell me, "These two kids are always fighting, but they cannot stay away from one another. They keep seeking one another out." That's not surprising if you understand that they are recreating the roles they play in their families. And what about the bystanders and the followers? Accustomed to those roles at home, they may replay them in the classroom. The teacher intuitively tries to get a child who is a follower to be the leader sometimes, or tells the habitual mover that it is time for another child to suggest a game.

Understanding Independent School Parents

Whether teachers are aware of it or not, they are always doing a kind of corrective family therapy, giving children opportunities to move away from their established family psycho-political roles. A mover at home gets the chance to be a follower during the school day; the bystander at home can try out her skills at initiation in her fourth grade classroom. Such opportunities help children grow. At times, of course, adults are induced by a child's behavior to enter into his or her family dramas; without knowing it we play the role of some family member, sometimes in negative ways.

Parents' Fears

One of the most surprising discoveries teachers make is to realize that parents are frightened of them — not every day, of course, and not all parents. Nevertheless, the fear is there. This latent fear, often denied and only painfully approached, can infect the relationship between independent school teachers and independent school parents. It can be difficult for a young teacher to see the insecurity in an older, accomplished professional person. It is only over time that teachers come to understand that insecurity is part and parcel of being a parent. Even the most powerful and accomplished parent fears the power of his or her child's teachers.

Can that really be so? I believe it can, and I have three reasons for saying so. First, parents have told me about their fears. Second, I have seen fear on the faces of parents who have never articulated it. Third, I am an

A Matter of Style: Understanding Family Differences

independent school parent and I have always valued, admired, *and* feared the extraordinary power that teachers have over my child's life — and therefore over me.

As soon as my children began attending preschool, I found that I both appreciated the love that teachers lavished on my children and I feared their judgment of me. Why? Because I was an amateur struggling with the job that teachers do professionally every day. But the awareness of my limitations was only one of a number of fears that all parents bring to the parent-teacher relationship.

I have identified six fears that gnaw at parents when they come in to see their child's teachers.

1. *Parenting is inherently difficult and no one is experienced at it.* The first child in a family makes her competent parents feel helpless, and every subsequent child challenges parents in new and unexpected ways. As Anonymous once said, "Anything which parents have not learned from experience, they can now learn from their children." All parents are amateurs and they know it.

2. *Your child-rearing mistakes (and your character flaws) are on display through your child's behavior in ways you cannot know.* Every teacher, without exception, has drawn negative conclusions about the character of parents whom he or she has never met, based on the behavior of their child. It

is impossible to be in a classroom without judging parents from a distance. Parents are aware of that. When my daughter was not yet three, my wife and I attended our first teacher conference with her gifted preschool teachers, Nancy and Vicki. After they had said many nice things about Joanna, there was The Pause that all parents dread. Nancy said, "You know, she is a terrible tease." My wife looked at me, and I looked at my shoes. There was nothing else to do. I knew from whom my daughter had learned to tease, because I had learned it from my father. My character was on display in front of my child's teachers: a very exposing moment.

3. *Every parent is trapped by hope, love — and anxiety.* Parents are unavoidably vulnerable with respect to their children. I had an anxious friend who, after her first child was born, called her pediatrician twice a day for about two months. Finally, the pediatrician's secretary called her and asked her to come in for an appointment (no mention of the baby). He sat down with her and said, "Mrs. Smith, you have given birth to a child. You have opened yourself up to a lifetime of anxiety. You have to *pace* yourself." I believe that all parents are pacing themselves with respect to their anxieties. And there are times when your worry breaks through in ways you cannot control.

4. *In important ways, you may not know as much about your child as his or her teacher does.* As children

grow older and more complex they do not reveal all facets of their personality to their parents. Adolescents, especially, show their teachers sides of themselves that they deliberately hide from their moms and dads. When parents sit down with teachers, they may have the uncomfortable feeling that they're missing a crucial piece of information — and they're probably right.

5. *Teachers have immense power over children's lives.* Teachers have the power and opportunity to praise, to support or to criticize. Parents are keenly aware of teacher power, because as children they too had teachers who made them feel wonderful or terrible.

6. *Parents may feel trapped by and with their child's school.* Schools are not commodities and are not easily changed, even when things are going badly for a child. For reasons of geography, lack of good public school options, the child's friendships (or the parents!) there may be no other options.

If parents come to their child's school feeling amateurish, anxious, ignorant and trapped, they naturally reach for the set of skills that makes them successful in the "outside" world. Independent school parents usually have those skills in abundance, but when they're displayed in a school conference these qualities can be unhelpful at best and destructive at worst. I once had an entrepreneurial parent come to me for help with his ninth grade son. The dad made a business presentation about the boy that took up the entire hour we had together. It was an articulate, polished, forceful sales presentation. It made me want to shout, "But we're not buying your child. He's already here!"

To regain my patience with this business-oriented father I had to remind myself that at times of stress lawyers act like lawyers (and sometimes make threatening statements), mental health professionals act like mental health professionals (and cannot stop analyzing everything and everybody), and so on. Even educators, when they're in a parental role, tend to make suggestions about the curriculum that irritate classroom teachers. Even when parents know that their skills are not appropriate to the educational situation, they cannot stop themselves. It can be difficult for teachers to remember that this behavior happens because of fear on the parent's part.

Teachers' Fears

Teachers bring their own set of fears to the parent-teacher conference that is the mirror image of worries that burden parents.

1. *Teaching, like parenting, is an inherently difficult job that is hard to measure and intensely personal.* You can never, like a businessperson, point to your "bottom line" and say, "My teaching is up 43 percent over last year." There are so many variables in teaching: the complexity of the students and the families they come from, the

variation of learning styles in every classroom, the interpersonal chemistry among children and between the students and the teacher, the time of year, etc., etc. You can have brilliant ideas, design the best lesson plan, arrive at the classroom full of energy—and have your class destroyed by an angry boy whose parents are getting divorced. No teacher has the power to guarantee the outcomes he or she wants. But when things do not go right in class, you cannot say to an unhappy parent, "You should have seen my class *last* year. It was amazing." This leaves teachers feeling vulnerable in front of parents.

2. *Teachers' faults are on display in front of the distorting eyes of children.* Teaching is a public, exposing job and the child audience is not always appreciative or kind. Teachers may not want to think about it, but they are discussed in many homes many evenings, and the discussions are based on the sometimes distorted impressions of children. So when a set of parents comes to talk to you, you don't know much about what they have heard about you from their kids — but you can be sure that it was not always what you would regard as accurate or true.

3. *You teach well and effectively but you do not always get the credit you deserve.* A good teacher creates a setting where the children star. Parents are all too ready to see the child as the creator of success ("She's so brilliant!"), not the teacher. I think all

teachers must wonder if the hard, often invisible work they do is going to be appreciated. The social critic Jacques Barzun has written, "Teaching is not a lost art, but respect for it is a lost tradition."

4. *Teachers are not accorded enough respect in our culture.* The fact that teachers are underpaid relative to other professions in a capitalistic society is a tangible sign of cultural disrespect. It is difficult not to feel that in a personal way. When you sit down across from a parent who makes not just twice or three times what you do, but two hundred times what you do, it's bound to make you feel somewhat small. Many independent school parents, whatever their income, are high-status in a variety of ways. "What can I say to some of these important parents? I see them on TV every night," a young teacher in Washington, DC, asked me once. I remember being a 25-year-old teacher at a school outside Boston, teaching psychology — including child development — to high school students. On parent-teacher conference day, one of the parents walked into my classroom – T. Berry Brazelton, full professor of pediatrics at the Harvard Medical School and best-selling author of millions of books on... child development. I must have looked terrified because Dr. Brazelton spoke first. "Don't worry," he said, "I know everything about infants and nothing about adolescents. Please tell me about my daughter." Not every

prestigious parent is so willing to create a level playing field for a young teacher.

5. *Every teacher who has been in the profession for even a few years has been attacked by at least one parent.* A veteran teacher, after describing a parent who had verbally attacked him 12 years earlier, said to me, "Every time a parent comes through the door, I wonder, 'Could this be one of those?'" That teacher is a victim of what psychologists call "one-time learning." That one parent had made him slightly wary of all parents. I worry about this phenomenon, because I do not want teachers to generalize from one exotic and terrible parent to all parents.

6. *Teachers fear that parents' influence with school administrators means that their jobs could be at risk.* One of the most damaging myths in independent schools is that parents, especially wealthy parents or board-member parents, can pick and choose teachers. In my 20-plus years in schools, I have visited only a handful of schools where I thought parents had that kind of power. When parents do have a say in personnel matters it demoralizes the faculty and completely undermines the head of school. It is a terrible situation but it is *extremely rare* — and it never occurs in a school with a good teacher evaluation program.

Understanding Independent School Parents

Moving Beyond Fear

I have worked with independent school teachers for many years and I have been struck by their sense of vulnerability about parents. The most obvious reason is that independent school teachers, unlike their tenured counterparts in the public sector, have only a one-year contract. No doubt that is a factor in their sense of vulnerability but I do not think it is the fundamental one. At the deepest level, I think that teachers are vulnerable precisely because they are full of feeling. Teachers must always be open to and to a certain extent identify with the vulnerable emotions of children. That openness, which I admire, can make a teacher appear "soft" when he or she is with a tough, bottom-line parent who wants his son in AP Biology so that the boy can go to an elite college — no matter how much his son struggled in previous science classes. The teacher is inevitably in the position of advocating for the child to the parent, and sometimes contradicting a parent who thinks he knows what the "real world" is all about or thinks of himself as a customer who must be satisfied. This can be a tricky position that leaves a teacher feeling out on a limb.

There are a number of ways in which teachers can get past their fear. The three most important structural cures are: good administrative leadership; an effective teacher evaluation program; and a board of trustees that does not meddle or micromanage. If heads of school make it clear that they are going to protect teachers and they and their administrators do so visibly, the impact on teacher

32

sense of safety is palpable. If administrators do not provide the essential protection, teachers will fear parents.

A rigorous, professional evaluation program offers powerful protection for teachers. A good evaluation is a teacher's friend, so it has always baffled me why teachers dislike evaluation. If you have two or three strong evaluations in your file you have nothing to fear from an irrational parent. Your character, the ongoing quality of your work, and your success with students will be documented and can stand up to the idiosyncratic negative reaction of one parent or one child.

Finally, boards of trustees have to stay out of the hiring and firing process in a school. If they do not, faculty members will become demoralized and frightened, certain that their administrators cannot protect them — and they will be right. The school may appear to be stable and thriving but over time it will lose its strongest teachers; it will end up with only its most political and most obedient teachers, the ones who cultivate a following among parents and the ones who always trim their sails in response to parental whims and desires. If a board wants a strong school it must hire a strong head and let him or her evaluate and protect his or her teachers.

Chapter Three

Developing Alliances: Relationships with Reasonable Parents

The single most important step toward safety for a teacher is to make a strong alliance with the 95 percent of parents who are reasonable. There are an infinite number of ways to make positive alliances with people and I could not possibly catalogue them here. But I do not need to. Teachers are "people" people and their own hearts and common sense make them yearn for good connections with children. They also want to connect with parents and it is only discomfort, wariness and fear that get in the way. I say "only" because with 95 Percenters, wariness and fear are unnecessary, if you do a few basic things. (With 5 Percenters, wariness and fear are essential.)

Over the years, I have boiled all my advice about making alliances with parents into three suggestions. I believe that if you follow them your relationships with parents will improve. No, I'll go beyond that. I'll make an outrageous claim. If you follow these suggestions, your alliances with parents will be stronger, your connections to children will be warmer, your students will perform better, and you will like your job more. So here goes:

Understanding Independent School Parents

1. Ask parents about their hopes and fears for their children.

All parents are gripped by their love for their children, the dreams they dream on their behalf, and especially by their worries about them. You cannot really understand the psychology of any human being without knowing what he or she is hoping for and worrying about. I don't know how many times a parent has told me, "A mother is only as happy as her unhappiest child." Mothers say it about themselves; men say it about their wives and imply it about themselves. If that is true, then it is important for a teacher to know something about a parent's yearnings and disappointed hopes, which I will call fears. Ask them, and listen to their answers.

Because I am a psychologist, and as a result of my personality and my training, I have always felt drawn to know what people most aspire to and, by the same token, what terrifies them most. It is natural for me to ask such things. Teachers do not necessarily imagine that interviewing a parent about his or her fears is part of their job description. I know it sounds so like a "shrink" to recommend that a teacher look deep into the eyes of a parent and utter the words "hopes and fears." But I am not saying that a teacher should act like a therapist. A teacher can go up to a parent on the sidelines of a soccer field and ask, "How's the year going for Suzie? Is it what she was hoping for?" Stand and listen and you will learn a lot, not just about Suzie's hopes, but the parent's hopes as well.

Now, here is the magic in my advice: It is enough to listen, perhaps to ask a follow-up question, but mainly just be an active listener. Sometimes teachers think they have to be brilliant, that they have to give advice or solve a problem. That tendency comes from having to wrap things up at the end of a class or the end of a semester, to draw meaning out of chaos, to highlight the lesson. But you do not have to do that when you ask another person about their hopes and fears. All you have to do is receive a parent's experience of his or her child and the feelings that surround that experience.

One Cambridge parent, who sent her son to a wonderful Quaker school, said to me, "Whenever I go to my child's school, all the teachers spend the time trying to convince me that the curriculum is marvelous and that they know what they're doing. What bothers me is that they do not seem at all interested in what *I* know about my child."

If a parent feels like that when she walks away from a conversation with a teacher, a precious opportunity has been lost. I hope you will remember that before you embark on an extended explanation of or defense of your curriculum and teaching methods. It is likely that a parent's questions, even her apparently attacking inquiries, arise from her own worries about her child. Better to ask her what she knows about her child than to tell her what you know about your own curriculum.

Once a parent tells a teacher something meaningful about his hopes and fears for his child, his relationship with the teacher will strengthen. Even a 5- or ten-minute conversation will begin to build the foundation of an alliance, a bridge between you that will support some weight. A parent will experience, for the few minutes you listen to his hopes and fears, your empathy, your interest, and your full attention. That counts for a lot.

Since most parents never see a teacher teach, they usually judge him or her on two criteria: whether or not their child appears to thrive in that teacher's class, and their own personal impressions of the teacher. I believe that most parents are more influenced by the latter than the former because a direct impression is always more powerful than a vicariously experienced story — even from one's child. Indeed, if a parent has come to trust a teacher through a "hopes and fears" conversation, he or she is likely to listen to the child's description of some heinous teacher crime and say, "That's odd. That doesn't jibe with my impression. I thought your teacher was a very reasonable and understanding person." That can only happen if the teacher and the parent have had a meaningful conversation, one about the parent's greatest yearnings and deepest fears. If it should happen that the child grows critical or there is an impasse of some kind, the parent is willing to trust the teacher until things are worked out. They have built a bridge between them that will support some weight.

If a parent tells you in September that he is worried that his seventh grade son, once a talented A student, is now being influenced too much by friends who are "underachievers" you can take that explanation into account as you get to know the boy. There may be other explanations, or the parental concern may be well founded. In either case, if you have to call in early November to notify the father that his son is in disciplinary trouble for pulling some prank with a bunch of friends, or is not getting anything done in study hall, you are on much firmer ground if you begin the conversation with, "You know, ever since you told me of your worries I have been watching your son with his friends. I now have to conclude that you are right. They are pulling each other down. They are the cause of his getting nothing done in study hall, and regrettably, he is the reason *they* aren't getting anything done either." How much better to start a call that way than to have to call and say, "Hello, we've never met, but I have to inform you that your son and his friends are not working at all in study hall." No matter how diplomatically or how gently you introduce this news, if you have no prior relationship the parent is going to become a bit defensive. We all do when we hear here something critical, or even vaguely reproachful, about our child.

If you and the parent have a pre-existing relationship, even if it consists only of the one "hopes and fears" conversation that I have suggested, it will make an extraordinary difference not only in how the conversation goes but also in how you and the parent feel about each other.

In the past, I have divided the participants at the Westtown Teachers Seminar into two groups and asked them to do the hopes and fears exercise, wearing either their parent hat or their teacher hat. The "teachers" are instructed to ask only the "hopes and fears" question and the "parents" are instructed to react naturally as parents. Invariably, the pairs come back liking one another. "What a smart parent, he knew so much about his daughter." "What an amazing teacher, I wish that my son could be in her class." Very often a parent will have cried, and the teacher will have identified with the parent's love and the parent's concern. It is quite astonishing how quickly a relationship forms between two adults when it is centered on a parent's feelings for his or her children.

Bart Dankarts, a Westtown alumnus, wrote me a letter in which he described the impact of asking the parents at the International School of Brussels the "hopes and fears" question at parent-teacher conferences in October. "In every one of my conferences I asked the hopes and fears question," he reported. "The parents were surprised, because the convention in Europe is to go over the report card in the conference, but they were all glad to answer the question. I came away from the conferences liking the parents a lot better than I had before and the unexpected outcome was that some students who had never felt close to me before that time began to talk to me more openly after those conferences."

Why did this happen? We can speculate parents had gone home and said to their children, "We really liked that Mr. Dankarts. He seems like a very understanding man." How did the parents know that? They had talked to him about their yearnings and fears and he had listened with respect and attention.

2. Say something that claims a child.

Too many teachers think that a parent is going to be won over with a recitation of a child's strong points. By all means, if a teacher "just loves" a child in her class, and can say so with authentic enthusiasm, he or she should do just that. That warms any parent's heart. More to the point — and something a teacher can do with any child and any parent — is to say something that "claims" the child.

What do I mean by that? Let me tell you a story I have been using for years; I have never come up with a better one. When my daughter was in third grade in a fine, progressive independent school she was floundering badly. She was learning disabled and the open classroom that had so appealed to my wife and me did not provide her with enough structure. When we met with Joanna's third grade teachers in March, they said a number of things which I remember as: "Joanna doesn't finish anything, she's always wandering around, she's always in the bathroom or wanting to guide prospective parents around the school." Whatever the teachers meant to say, it sounded to us like a laundry list of Joanna's defects, with no plan to help her. We decided to take Joanna out and place her in our local public school, which enjoyed a great reputation for its special education and especially for the coordination between mainstream classroom teachers and resource room teachers. Joanna was furious with us; she resented losing her familiar surroundings and her friends. We were at sea, as well, because we were products of private and parochial education; neither of us knew the public system very well.

In the third week of October we went to our parent-teacher conference with Joanna's new teacher, Mrs. Black. Mrs. Black, whom we had barely met before, said the following: "I like to think of Joanna as being like a butterfly. She alights on one thing, and then another, and another, and another. My job as her teacher is to persuade her that it is going to be all right; she can stay with something and finish it."

My wife and I began to tear up. We loved the teacher instantly. I wanted to kiss Mrs. Black's feet! Why? Because in three sentences she went to the heart of our daughter's learning difficulties and told us what she was going to do about them. She *claimed* our child. The use of the butterfly analogy was lovely, but that was not the essence of what she said. She accurately described my daughter's defensive style in the classroom and then said what her job as a teacher was going to be. No guarantees. No sugarcoating. Yet she conveyed that she was on top of things.

Ninety-five percent of parents will be extremely grateful if you can claim their child in this way. Parents want their children to be known, to be cared about, and to be educated. Mrs. Black gave us that assurance in three sentences.

Will everyone be grateful if you say something to claim their child? Of course not. Five Percenters will think you have missed the boat no matter what you say. So my advice is to be as fearless and accurate as you can be and be prepared for the 5 Percenters to quibble with you. But if you have already asked them something about their hopes and fears, you may have been able to glean something that they recognize and identify with, at least for the moment.

3. Run a professional meeting.

In my view, independent schools are service organizations. But some parents get confused and think they are buying a commodity when they pay that tuition bill. I'm thinking of the father who said, "I didn't send my son to a school like this to get B's." He, like a minority of parents, thought he was paying for a *product*: A's for his son, A's that would lead inexorably to Wesleyan or Harvard. But no parent is paying tuition for that, because educators cannot promise to deliver that product. What parents are paying for is an education for their children, no matter how it turns out. There are no money-back guarantees in independent schools. Parents pay for small class size, good relationships between students and teachers, an enriched environment, and high morale. Everyone involved hopes that all of that will turn into something good for the child — but there is no guarantee.

However, there is one aspect of service to which a parent is entitled: a well-run parent-teacher conference. In my experience as an independent school parent, that is not something that one can count on getting. When I had a clinical practice, and cancelled a morning of patients to go to my child's school conferences, I found many of the meetings were run sloppily. They started late, the teachers were vague and disorganized, and the meetings never had a decent wrap-up. A teacher might look up, suddenly seeing another set of parents through the glass of the classroom door and say, "Whoops! We've run out of time. There's another family waiting." No matter how likable a teacher, no matter how good with my child, the parent-teacher conference itself was unprofessional and I came away from it with a less-than-complimentary view of the teacher's organization and planning.

Teachers need to remember that the parent-teacher conference may be the only way a parent has of assessing his or her professionalism. There is never enough time, the setting may be awkward (those tiny chairs), but it is an important opportunity. Therefore, teachers need to run a meeting that begins and ends on time, where an agenda is created at the beginning and reviewed at the end. For example, a teacher needs to say at the beginning, "We only have 15 minutes to discuss Johnny, and that's not a lot of time. Are there some particular concerns you would like me to address?" A parent might demur, saying, "We just want to hear you talk about how he is doing." I don't think a teacher should accept that as the complete agenda. "Of course I will talk about how he is doing, but aren't there some particular concerns you have that I could address?" (Notice how the teacher can use the agenda-setting part of the meeting to elicit some "hopes and fears"?)

Once an agenda has been created, the teacher should stick to it and not digress. There are precious few minutes of communication time in these parent-teacher conferences. At the end the teacher should say, "Did you learn what you came to learn from me? Do you have the answers to some of your questions?"

If the parents say, yes, they have gotten the answers to their questions, then they leave as satisfied customers — and they will stay that way. How do we know that? Because they will have heard the world's foremost authorities (namely themselves) say out loud, "Yes, thank you. We now understand why Suzie struggles in Chemistry." Suzie may not be getting an A, but the parent has some understanding about why. Her B or a C is tolerable, and the teacher will not be irrationally blamed for it, if the parents' questions about their daughter's struggle have been answered thoughtfully.

If the parents say, "No, we did not learn what we had hoped to learn from this meeting," a teacher should never be defensive. Fifteen minutes is precious little time to understand the complex business of a child's cognitive development, academic style, and motivation. It is astonishing that parents ever go away satisfied from a 15-minute or even a half-hour conference. Therefore, it is no one's fault when not all the business has been done. A teacher needs to say, "Okay, we should then schedule another meeting. How soon do you want that to be? And who else should we have at the meeting? Would you like the middle school director here?" Parent-teacher meetings are a service, all parents are entitled to receive them, and no teacher needs to feel bad about that. A need to schedule another meeting is not a failure on anyone's part.

Understanding Independent School Parents

So run a professional meeting. If you do, you will earn the respect of parents who themselves run many meetings a week, either in their professional and business lives or in their volunteer lives. Independent school parents expect a professional meeting and they know it when they experience it. The disorganized, amateur meeting should be the rare exception.

I guarantee that if you ask about hopes and fears and then really listen, if you say something to claim the child, and if you run a professional meeting, 95 percent of the parents you deal with will relax. They will trust you, their beloved child's teacher, and will think they have made a brilliant decision to be paying thousands of dollars in tuition. They will feel well looked after and they will trust that their child is well looked after too.

Chapter Four

From Bad to Worse: Three Types of "5 Percenter" Parents

Who are the parents who scare, terrify, frustrate, confuse and break the hearts of teachers? I believe there are three types of particularly difficult parents in independent schools: threatening-abusive parents; anxious-incompetent parents; and denying and unresponsive parents. Teachers often fear intimidating-threatening parents. They find themselves baffled and overwhelmed by anxious-incompetent parents. And they stand helpless and angry when denying and unresponsive parents refuse, over many years, to get the help for their children that is so obviously needed.

Threatening-abusive parents use power to try to control meetings or to get what they want from the system. A father, glancing at his watch, once said to me at the beginning of a meeting: "I am an important international entrepreneur and it was extremely difficult for me to get to this meeting." We had called the meeting because his daughter was in such chronic distress at school. He was outraged and he let us know that by emphasizing his importance.

Parents who talk about the tuition money (For example, "I pay your salary," "You work for me," or "For all the tuition I pay, I would have thought that… ") or parents who attack a teacher's professionalism are the ones I call threatening and abusive. Once you recognize that you're in a meeting with such a parent, you must stop being as trusting, generous-hearted and intent on problem solving as you would be with a 95 Percenter. You must be more guarded, more careful and stay ready to say, "I do not think this meeting is productive. Perhaps we should end it and reschedule when the director of the Lower School can be with us." If the parent charges ahead, continuing in a threatening fashion, the teacher should say, "I don't feel comfortable in this meeting any longer. I insist that we must stop today and reschedule for another time." Power tactics are the only way to counter some power-oriented people. They will either stop when they hit a clear limit, or they will continue; in which case, the teacher needs to end the meeting. It is *never* a mistake for a teacher to end a meeting in which he or she feels unsafe.

Anxious-incompetent parents tend to flood a teacher with their worries, or attempt to turn their child over to the teacher to be raised. "Would you talk to her about the way she dresses?" asks the mother of an eighth-grade girl, "She doesn't listen to me at all." This is the kind of mother who continues to buy her daughter clothes that are too small and too revealing. This is a mother who drives her daughter to school in the morning, and then calls the middle school director to say, "I just don't know what to do about the way she dresses." Obviously, a mother with courage would not drive her daughter to school unless she were dressed properly; the overwhelmed mother gives in at every step.

Teachers who get sucked in (the term in psychology is "inducted") by the family neurosis are never given a full license to cure the problem. Everything the teacher does will be met with anxiety and more overwhelmed feelings. Ultimately, the teacher may herself become overwhelmed with phone calls. I have spoken to teachers who have gotten upwards of a hundred calls and e-mails *before Christmas* from an endlessly anxious parent.

It is wise to recognize that you cannot cure a parent's endless anxiety by taking one fruitless phone call after another. After you have offered the developmental explanation — "Many sixth graders get caught up in mean Instant Messaging" — that has neither given the parent the courage to help limit her daughter's internet use nor reassured her that everything is going to be all right, you may have to ask, "Nothing I have done so far seems to have made things better or reassured you in any way. Is there any way that I could reassure you?" The honest answer, if the mom is a true 5 Percenter, is probably, "No, no one ever has been able to reassure me. I'm just chronically anxious. I should probably get psychotherapy for myself, but it is more interesting for me to get over-involved in my daughter's life and worry constantly." Wouldn't it be great if parents really said things like that?

Because teachers tend to be generous-hearted problem solvers, anxious-incompetent parents can sometimes be the toughest for them to manage. Teachers keep throwing themselves back into the arena, hoping to make everyone feel better. That simply does not work with someone suffering from a depressive or anxious mental disorder. When you clean up one source of suffering, there is always another waiting to fill that space. I don't like to see teachers take on a lot of someone else's anxiety, yet I have seen it many times in schools. Some of the most admirable teachers have a desire to rescue which makes them go much farther than they should down the path of endless anxiety with an overwhelmed parent. At some point, a parent like that needs to be turned over to the administration so the teacher can return to her classroom with a clear mind.

Finally, there are the denying and unresponsive parents, the rare but truly malevolent parents who *never* get the help that their children truly need. The teachers see the child clearly, the administrators do, the recommendations are sound and humane, yet the parents refuse. For reasons of their own mental illness, their own terrible marriages, their own self-absorption, or their own destructive psychological projections onto their children, some parents harm their children. When I worked at a boarding school we once had a boy who was found in a bathtub holding a knife to his throat, saying he was going to kill himself. We took him to the emergency room, which did not keep him, and then called his parents to come and get him. His mother, herself a physician, called the next morning to say that a family friend, a psychiatrist, had evaluated him and that he was fine. They would be driving him back that afternoon. It was the school that had to say no, that their son was not safe in a boarding situation.

Parents like this do not want anyone to get in the way. When teachers encounter such parents, it takes a long time for them to really believe that the parents cannot or will not act in their child's best interest. Yet it is certainly true that some parents destroy their children right in front of our eyes. All we can do is call the state protective agency if there is a case of abuse and neglect. Short of that, we can document in writing the difficulties of the child, the recommendations of the school, and the continued unresponsiveness of the parents. I have seen parents whose practice was to nod and say "yes" in school meetings, only to return home and do nothing about the recommendations. These are the true heartbreakers of the school world.

Part Two: What Teachers Can Do

By Alison Fox Mazzola, M.Ed.

Chapter Five

A Good Fit: Seek a Supportive School

We wrote this book to give you ideas for working with difficult parents in any teaching environment. But if you are working with difficult parents and the administration of your school is so swayed by their ideas that you end up getting beaten down by both parents and school, you're not advancing your career or self-esteem by staying there. You deserve an environment where you will be supported, trusted, and respected. Difficult parents are hard enough to work with without having to go it alone. So position yourself in a place where you will get some support. Not every school is right for every student and not every school is right for every teacher. If your philosophy does not match that of the school or if your teaching style is radically different from the teachers who are already there, you are going to make your job harder. Get yourself into a position of strength.

Early on in my career I had an experience that I was too new to teaching to understand was quite bizarre. At the time, I was so grateful to have a teaching job that I was reluctant to do anything to "rock the boat." In retrospect, I should have been a lot more assertive and asked to be treated more respectfully. I was at a school that was less than 10 years old. The founder had opened the school with four students. He was teacher, janitor, chef, counselor, and admissions director all at once. By the time I arrived, he had narrowed his job description to "Head of School," but still felt responsible for all aspects of the school's operation. At that time his main focus was gaining and keeping students — and students seemed to be harder to come by than teachers. The head's bias in that regard became clear as I worked with one family.

One week in September I left a faculty meeting early to meet with Judith Meyer's family. Judith was a shy, quiet, large-eyed third grader. She always came to school impeccably dressed and rarely spoke. She did have some friends and usually enjoyed reading with them at recess.

Her family wanted to meet with me about the math curriculum. They had been at the school for a while so they were familiar with the program but were surprised to hear that the Chicago Math Program called for the use of calculators on occasion. They asked that their child have alternate work at these times. Easy enough, I thought.

Two weeks later I gave a homework assignment in which the children were to look up unfamiliar words from the novel *Sarah, Plain and Tall* and write down the definitions. I ran into Mrs. Meyer in the hallway and she told me that the words were completely inappropriate for third grade and she did not like the homework assignment so she had created one of her own. She also told me that she had taken home copies of all the books we would be using for the year so that she and her husband could review them.

I went to the head of school and mentioned this since her action left me without enough books for each student. He told me to "make do" so that that family could have their own copies.

Three weeks later our class went to the Museum of Science to see the exhibits that related to our study of plants. Judith's parents wouldn't let her come to school that day because of the field trip. When I asked Mrs. Meyer why Judith stayed home she said, "She needed to learn something, unlike what goes on here every day."

Again, I went to the head of school. The family seemed so unhappy and I thought he should know. I also hoped that he could talk with them and reassure them that the curriculum was well thought out and appropriate for third graders. He planned a meeting with the family and I was relieved.

At the meeting, however, they discussed vowels! I was teaching at the time the meeting occurred, but I was called in to it and told by the head of school that the family would like their child to be learning to read from the McGuffy Readers. (Our school didn't have any, and I later found out that they were used in the early 1900s.) I was also told that I shouldn't be taking the children to the computer lab.

A few weeks later the head came into my class while I was teaching and told me, and the whole class, that the Meyer family was thinking of leaving and asked me what I had done. I was shocked at his lack of support and the impropriety of discussing the situation in front of the students.

Understanding Independent School Parents

After he left it became clear to me that I was not going to feel successful in this environment. The head was not supporting my teaching or supporting the program he had set up for me to teach. In addition, he was scaring the children by coming in and yelling at me in front of them. He shared information with them that should have been for adults only. I began looking for another job — but I also knew I owed it to my students to finish out the year with them.

Before the school year ended I was walking down the hall with my teaching partner. It was the day after re-enrollment agreements were due. Three students in our group of 40 hadn't turned theirs in. The head of school stood over us and shouted, "Why are three of your students leaving? What did you do?" I knew then that even if I didn't find another job I would leave that school.

I had come to realize that the head wanted to keep the Meyer family and felt it was my job to do whatever was necessary to make that happen. In doing so, he was willing to bend the educational philosophy of the school and place the family's nonsensical educational demands above those of his teachers.

In other schools where I have worked, the administration will support a teacher in front of students, parents, and other teachers. If they need to, administrators will speak with the teacher in private about something they feel he or she could change. But they always support the teacher publicly. In this school,

A Good Fit: Seek a Supportive School

I was not supported publicly or privately. It was time to find a place where I could gain some more respect.

Luckily, I did find another job for the following year at a different school and was excited to begin again. At my new school we had our first set of conferences in mid-September. All was going well until one mother entered my classroom. Mrs. Tan drove a red, convertible sports car. She had her own parking space reserved in the school parking lot. It seemed that she was on every committee in the school. Everyone knew her. But I was new.

When Mrs. Tan came for her first conference, we chatted cordially for a few minutes and then she accused me of hitting her child. I was shocked at her accusations and quite shaken. Somehow I was able to end the conference professionally, but after the mother left, I wept. I thought I had finally found a school where I would be safe and here was this woman who had made an untrue, but potentially career-ending accusation.

The most difficult thing was not that she had made it but that no one could know that there was *no* possibility that the accusation was true. I hadn't been at the school long enough to prove myself yet — and the head of my previous school certainly wasn't going to vouch for me! I didn't have videotapes in my room to prove I hadn't done it. Outside of my demonstration lesson, I hadn't even been observed yet for people to see my demeanor with the children.

Understanding Independent School Parents

I worriedly went to the head of our division and recounted my story. "Don't worry, Alison," he said, "I know you didn't do it." I looked up incredulously. How did he know? To this day I still don't know why he had so much faith in me. But he did, and that made all the difference.

That administrator must have known that the mother's accusations were untrue because he had carefully chosen to hire me. He had visited me at my previous school and realized that I had a rapport with the children. He had been part of an interview team of 12 people who interviewed me two different times. After offering me the job, he also called me to talk to me about what it was like to teach at his school and why he thought I would like it. He had done his homework. By the time I started working at the school, he knew me fairly well and other teachers in the school community had gotten to know me, too. They trusted that I would do a good job; they had faith in me. They also knew that my philosophy of teaching matched the school's philosophy and hitting students had no place in either.

I have been at the same school for quite a while now. The difficult parents haven't gone away but I know that if I act professionally there are people to back me up and support me along the way.

Chapter Six

The Biggest Challenge: Managing Difficult Parents

Through the years, I have worked with over four hundred families. I have found that the children who enter my door each morning present certain challenges, but my biggest challenges have been working with some of the adults who accompany them. When we begin the school year we need to get to know our students, to learn how each of them ticks. We need to figure out how to excite them, challenge them, and help them learn. We also must consider that each child is one piece of a whole family with whom we will be working the entire year. This means we also have to figure out the student's parents. How can I best communicate with this family? What does this family expect from the school this year? What values are important to this family? How important is it to them that their child does well? How do they define success in school?

In general as teachers, the number of one-on-one conversations we have with parents is surprisingly small. We don't get much information and yet we can only form impressions about each family based on what we know. These impressions help us begin the partnership. These impressions are confirmed or disproved as we move through the school year.

With a few families we develop a comfortable rapport. We can talk openly about their children and sometimes come to know these parents as friends. With most families we develop professional, effective communication. It may not always be smooth but for the most part, the parents' and the teacher's goals for the child are similar and all can work towards them together.

Then there are the 5 percent that Michael described in the first section of this book. In general, 5 percent of independent school parents are very challenging to work with. They test our patience and tact to the limit. They are irrational when it comes to their children and because of that, most of our usual methods for working with parents aren't successful. Some of them had poor experiences in school themselves and don't know how to interact successfully with the school or don't trust the teacher. Sometimes these parents have other issues such as guilt about going back to work, a divorce, or a serious illness. Sometimes these parents actually do have their own mental difficulties.

Around October it becomes clear to me who the members of the 5 percent will be for that year. I used to come home and sigh and moan that I had *another* difficult parent. Then one year my husband pointed out, "Why are you so surprised? Every year there is at least one." He had a point. When I stopped thinking that this might be the year without a challenging parent and instead recognized it was going to happen, it became less difficult to accept.

Five Percenter parents have accused me of not loving their child enough or of hitting their child; they have called me at 7 AM on Saturday to change a piano lesson scheduled to take place a week later; they have demanded my cell phone number so they could reach me on Sundays. They have called my classroom incessantly, told me I didn't understand what it was like to be a working mother, even though I am one, and have asked me to come to the airport with another copy of their child's homework when they forgot it.

What is the best way to handle these situations? How can teachers maintain their own boundaries and yet still extend themselves for their students? I have found a few things that have helped. Read on.

Document, Document, Document

When you are working with your students, but especially when you are working with a difficult parent, there is nothing more important you can do than document. Document the things the child does, document the communications you have with the parents, document the efforts you make to help the child. The primary reason for doing this is that you will be able to see a child's progress. You will also be able to check your perceptions against reality. (Has this parent really called me four times in the last week?) You will have a record of the efforts you have made with the student and with the parents. I used to think that writing things down and dating them wasn't very official. After all, there's no neutral observer verifying what I see. I have learned that it is enough to write it down and date it. (Contemporaneously noting what happens can even hold up in court if things get that far.)

Understanding Independent School Parents

To keep track of my students, I use two small loose-leaf binders — the size that holds half sheets of paper. I like the small ones because I can carry them around the classroom and not feel like they are obtrusive. In each binder I make a section for each student. In one binder I keep all my notes on the students. I have a page each for math, reading, writing, conferences, behavior, and "other." This is where I keep track of which book each child is reading, what story they are writing, and how they did in math that day. I write down if anything noteworthy happens at recess or during an academic time. I find it important to keep track of things on the playground as well as in the classroom because often a child will have difficulties that show up while playing in a less structured environment but not in the classroom. I also write down direct quotes from the students, like the day a second grader said, "How come in all the Cinderella stories we have read from the U.S. she has blonde hair and in all the ones from Asia she has black hair?" I also take detailed notes during conferences and phone conversations. All this information goes into this binder.

It sounds like this is time consuming but it really isn't. I take about 15 minutes each day to sit down and write notes in my binder. Sometimes I write notes in the middle of a lesson if I want to be sure to remember something a child said. Some days I have a lot to say about one child and nothing about another but I try to write something on each child each week.

In the second binder I keep all noteworthy e-mails. I print them out, fold them in half, punch holes in them, and stick them in the binder. I used to keep everything in the same binder but it became too full. Some of you may prefer to save e-mails electronically and eliminate the need for a second binder. These emails are really important to me. I am too worried that something will happen to the computer and the e-mails will disappear so I keep them in both places.

During the year I refer back to these binders time and time again as I speak with the family, help the child, and speak with administrators. At the end of the year I paper clip each child's pages together and file them to be saved for three years. I figure if I haven't needed them in three years then I am really done with them. This may sound excessive but you would be surprised how many times I have referred back to the notes. Teachers of students in the upper grades love it when they are having difficulty with a student or a parent and I pull out my notes from the year that student was with me and can share things that worked. I have also used them when administrators have asked me about certain families.

My notes have even come in handy years later. The most difficult parent I have ever encountered was eventually asked to leave our school. Two years later the family's youngest daughter was ready for kindergarten and they reapplied. When I heard that this parent was trying to reenter our school, I pulled together a 15-page document detailing every difficult interaction I had had with the family. This documentation was what the head and the board needed. After reviewing the school's experiences with this family, the school determined that the child's interest would be best served by a different school. The family has not reapplied but keeps telling other families that they will! And though it has been over five years and I have shredded my notes on the rest of their child's classmates, I still have all my notes on that family, just in case.

Keep in Touch

About ten years ago I was working in a public school in San Francisco. On Back-to-School Night, I stood alone in my room the whole evening. Not a single parent came to talk to me. I knew many of them were working second jobs and were unable to attend or didn't speak English and thus felt the evening wouldn't be useful. That evening made me realize how much I wanted to be in a school in which the parents were involved participants. I wanted parents who made sure their children finished their homework, who joined us on field trips, who came in to speak to the class about their experiences, and who followed what was happening in our classroom. I wanted to be able to say to a child, "I'm going to call your parents about this," and know that they would respond if I did. Mostly, I wanted to work as a team with parents to support the students. I wanted parents who felt it was important for their children to do well in school.

When I began working in independent schools I learned about communication with a capital "C." Independent school parents want to know everything that is going on with their child. Many of them would be happy if you would send home a report on their child every day. I have yet to hear from a parent that the six-page, narrative reports we write on the children in place of report cards at my school offer too much information.

Too Much — Way Too Much — Communication

Some parents have an insatiable desire to communicate with the teacher. They call the room five times a day or send a few three-page e-mails in one day. Sometimes the e-mails are about their child and sometimes they're about bigger school issues. These over-communicating parents are 5 Percenters. Among them was the Gotelli family. Just hearing their name sends shivers down my spine. This family turned my classroom upside down with their incessant need for communication.

I was teaching first grade in a suburban school. The school building was one story and sprawled over the area. Each grade had its own outdoor area where the students would have their morning recess, work in their class garden, and eat their lunch later in the day. The school building was only about 20 years old so it still felt fairly new and the play structures were still attractive and structurally sound. However, each year the school was replacing one or two play structures so that they wouldn't have to do them all at once at a later date. That year our grade was slated to receive a new structure. When the truck arrived in August, there was only one structure on it, not two. We were told that the factory only had one in stock and they didn't know when the next one would be available. I graciously offered that our class would be the one to wait for the other structure to arrive. We already had one that the students enjoyed. Sure, it wasn't shiny and new but it was still fun. I didn't think it would be a problem for us to wait a few more months. I also thought I could turn it into a learning opportunity and help the students learn that they could feel good about letting someone else go first.

When the children arrived in September, one mother immediately noticed that my class had not received its new play structure yet. When she asked about it I told her that we expected ours to arrive sometime during the school year but I didn't know exactly when. This mother quickly got in the habit of calling my room a few times a *day* to ask me why we didn't have the new play structure yet. Then she called the business office and asked them the same thing. They in turn called me and asked why this parent was so upset. Then she called the play-structure company who then called me to ask why this woman was involved. These calls went on for months. I grew worried that the structure company would boycott our school because this parent was driving them crazy. I stopped answering my classroom phone because she kept pulling me away from the students.

Eventually her son came to school one morning and announced to the class that I had tricked them and that the structure hadn't even been ordered. He said his mom had told him so! This news devastated the class and it took me a week to convince them that they could trust me again. Finally, after a few months, the structure arrived. Predictably, its arrival didn't do anything to boost the demanding mother's self-confidence.

The Biggest Challenge: Managing Difficult Parents

This mother pulled me away from my job of teaching students. I spent valuable classroom time on the phone with her, with the business office, and with the play-structure company. I also spent lots of classroom time discussing the structure with the students because one child was so upset about it.

This mother was so relentless that she made me question whether or not to be a teacher. I wanted to spend my time with students. I didn't want to spend my time calming angry mothers and vendors. I know now that I immediately should have referred her to an administrator. Seeking help from the administration earlier in the process would have meant that someone with more authority than I had could serve as a go-between and leave me the time and space to work with students. But as an inexperienced independent school teacher I thought her behavior was something I had to tolerate.

Share Good News

I sometimes wonder if that invasive mom would have calmed down if I had taken the initiative in communicating with her. One thing I do now that helps me considerably with many parents is send home a weekly letter. Each Friday I write two pages discussing what we have been learning that week. I talk about the big concepts I was teaching and I often include some quotes from the children to convey their reactions. Parents often hear about what their children did in school; my letter gives me a place to explain why it happened, and in adult terms. I also include detailed information about forms that need to be filled out, upcoming field trips, and other news.

With the advent of e-mail I have been able to send this communication weekly without much extra effort. Since parents know it is coming every Friday they are on the lookout for it. They read it and then if they have any further questions they contact me. This letter has saved time because parents no longer call me to find out when we are leaving on our field trip or which math lesson we did that week. It's all in the letter.

I also try and send one "good news" e-mail a day. It only takes about five minutes and parents love to get them. I pick a child in my class who did something noteworthy and write to their family about it. The parents are happy to get the e-mail and it helps build my relationship with the whole family. This is especially important at the beginning of the school year. Later, if I have to share some difficult news with a family, they will be better able to hear it after all the good news I have shared.

In some ways, e-mail has been a godsend for teachers. You can converse with parents on your own time. Since parents and teachers are with children at different times of day and evening, this flexibility is crucial. It also allows you to communicate a short message quickly and not get caught up in a long phone conversation when you have a class or are at home with your family.

The Biggest Challenge: Managing Difficult Parents

I used to think that e-mail was a good place for all communication. But I have come to see that while it is effective for sharing information, it does not work for discussions. After a difficult spring with one family I realized that e-mail cannot convey tone and thus comments can come across as biting when they are not meant that way. E-mail also does not convey body language or facial expressions, critical components of effective communication.

As busy teachers, it is hard to schedule yet another meeting when our work lives are already so full. However, a face-to-face meeting may save time in the long run as it is an opportunity to look a parent in the eyes, see their body language, and hear the tone in their voice. It is also an opportunity for them to see you as a person, experience your classroom, and get a sense of how you relate to other people, including their child. These things cannot be done over e-mail.

The Perils of E-Mail

These may sound like small issues — and they are when you are confirming the time of the class play. But e-mail discussion can get out of hand when it concerns a larger issue. Below are some e-mails I exchanged with a family before I learned my lesson about the perils of electronic communication. I kept trying to explain myself over e-mail to avoid scheduling another meeting into my busy day. Big mistake.

Understanding Independent School Parents

October 11
TO: Alison
FROM: Claudia
SUBJECT: Classroom visit

Hi Alison,
Each year I like to visit Madison's school for one whole day. I like to watch him in his classroom and go with him to his specialist classes. It gives me an opportunity to see how he is in class and what his different teachers are like. It also gives me an opportunity to think anew about whether we have chosen the right educational environment for him. I am eager to do this again this year. Please give me a few dates that would be convenient for you. Thank you.

Claudia

Madison was a youngster who had already been in two schools before he joined us in first grade. His mother did not work outside the home and spent lots of time with her only child. While she claimed that she loved our school's progressive philosophy, she was also concerned that Madison would not receive all the traditional skills he needed. She usually e-mailed me every other day about her son. I tried to explain our philosophy via e-mail.

The Biggest Challenge: Managing Difficult Parents

December 3
TO: Alison
FROM: Claudia
SUBJECT: Subtraction

You mentioned that Madison needs lots of practice when he is learning a new concept. You know, I don't find that to be the case at home. As you may know, I have 'home schooled' him in many subjects.

December 9
TO: Claudia FROM: Alison
SUBJECT: Learning how to learn

Claudia,
I do not feel that it is helpful for us to dissect Madison's attendance record to pinpoint exactly which days and lessons he missed. I am not looking for the specific facts he has learned. I am trying to figure out how he learns and thinks. As I mentioned, I am not so much concerned with the fact that he didn't know how to subtract two-digit numbers but more with if this might be an indicator of his learning style or even of a difficulty.

As a school, we do not believe in teaching children facts as an end in themselves. We want to teach them how to learn and how to think.

The material is a vehicle for this. Learning how to think and learn takes time and is not done in a lesson or a day. The fact that Madison knows the "right" spelling pattern is less useful to me than knowing how he learned it and what went through his mind as he did so. Of course, we want our students to learn the facts necessary to be educated but it is not useful if they know the facts but don't know how to use them.

I appreciate the fact that you do spend so much time working with him at home. This shows Madison that schoolwork is important. However, it also points to the fact that he needs time to practice skills. He practices them both at home and at school. I am often intrigued when we hit upon something that you haven't worked on at home. It is then that I really get to see Madison as a learner.

I invite you to come cook with us next week or go with us on our next field trip. I think that will help you get a better sense of the class and the other children. We are doing so much more here than worksheets and independent work. The children are learning how to learn.

Alison

December 9
TO: Alison
FROM: Claudia
SUBJECT: Practicing at home

Alison,
Your last e-mail did not make sense to me, Madison and I NEVER do academic work at home. Where did you get this from?

The Biggest Challenge: Managing Difficult Parents

January 10
TO: Alison
FROM: Claudia
SUBJECT: Madison prefers to work alone

...From what Madison has told me, he is being asked to work with other children to solve problems in math. Are you trying to teach math or are you trying to teach social skills? It is very challenging for Madison to be doing both at the same time and I just don't understand why you are doing this.

January 10
TO: Claudia
FROM: Alison
SUBJECT: RE: Madison prefers to work alone

Dear Claudia,
Yes, we are trying to teach interpersonal skills along with math. The children do need to learn to work with other children. Yes, I told Madison that he needed to work with Aidan for 10 minutes and give it a try. He had not been paired with Aidan before in any subject and didn't yet know how it would work out. He needs to be responsible for letting me know if he is having problems with his partner. This is his job. Another teacher sat with Madison and his partner for over twenty minutes. They were working very well together. ALL of the children use manipulatives to do subtraction problems. Madison benefited from this practice, especially where two trades were needed. This was not work that was below his level or unnecessary.

Learning to work with others is a crucial skill. Very few professionals work alone at their jobs. Madison needs to learn how to do this. He needs to learn to speak up when something is not working for him and he needs to speak up to his partner if he feels his partner is being unjust.

All people learn more by explaining their thinking to others and teaching others. We pair the children often in math (not every time) so that they can solidify their thinking by explaining it to others. This, along with partnership skills, is what we were working on yesterday.
Alison

Each morning when I got to school I had another e-mail from Claudia. In the spring she became convinced that the other children were hurting her child at recess. I calmly replied to her e-mail and by recess there was another from her. I replied and by lunchtime there was another and another by the end of the day. This went on every day! Again, I was trying to discuss a large issue through e-mail and would have saved myself time and difficulty if the mother and I had met in person.

As you have seen, I wrote this mother long, long e-mails trying to explain things to her—never a good idea with this shorthand form of communication. But it was so tempting to avoid having her criticize me to my face! I finally realized that she was going to keep e-mailing me no matter what I said. She never acknowledged that she had heard anything I said. I finally just started responding, "Thank you for your thoughts." She continued to e-mail — but I was no longer emotionally wrenched a few times a day. A face-to-face conversation would have answered a lot of her questions and calmed her down. She finally left the school, realizing that our environment was not a match for her expectations. This had been true from the start and even face-to-face communication would not have stopped it, but it would have calmed her down and saved me lots of time.

Our school has a policy that we respond to parent communication within 24 hours. I used to feel that this meant that I had to thoughtfully respond to each and every communication. While this is often a good idea, it can be tricky with difficult parents. In many instances, the most productive communication you can have with a difficult family is a short acknowledgment. If they send an e-mail, write back and say, "Thank you for your thoughts." That's it. Don't say any more. This way you won't be accused of ignoring their concerns but you also won't add fuel to their fire.

Effective E-Mailing

Having learned that discussions should not happen over e-mail, I invited Sarah's family to the classroom to discuss her recent homework.

May 6, 7:51 AM
TO: Janet
FROM: Alison
SUBJECT: Homework

Dear Janet,
As you know, the students are working on their final project of the year. This week's homework was a piece of that project. It seems that Sarah misunderstood the directions and I was

wondering if you could stop by the classroom when you come to pick her up so that we could all talk about it together.

Thank you. Alison

May 6 2:05 PM
TO: Alison
FROM: Janet
SUBJECT: Homework

Dear Alison,
Oh, dear, Sarah worked really hard on that homework. Can you give me some idea of what the difficulty was?

May 6 4:30 PM
TO: Janet
FROM: Alison
SUBJECT: Homework

Dear Janet,
The assignment was for the children to invent their own bread recipe. Since this is a culminating project of our study of bread, I wanted to see if the children could put together a recipe that included the main ingredients in bread (flour, water, salt, etc.) and if they could write a recipe that would actually work. Next week the students are going to bake their recipes and see if the bread is edible. Based on the notes on her homework, it looks like Sarah started with a recipe that someone else created and added cinnamon. The next step will be less meaningful to her if she already knows her recipe is going to work. Can we get together tomorrow after school and talk about this with Sarah? I know she worked hard on her homework but I'm wondering if

we can find a way to have her meet the goal of designing a recipe.

Alison

May 6 9:58 PM
TO: Alison
FROM: Janet
SUBJECT: Homework

Dear Alison,
I can see that Sarah interpreted the assignment differently but I can assure you that she still met your goals. Let's get together tomorrow afternoon and talk about it in person. I'll bring the cookbook that we started with so we can discuss it. Thank you for your understanding.

Janet

By getting together in person we were able to clear up the confusion about Sarah's homework. Her mother explained that she really had invented a whole new recipe and in the end she didn't need to redo the assignment. I wouldn't have known this if we hadn't talked about it. Meeting in person also gave me a chance to convey my understanding that Sarah had worked hard and help her mother see that I was not trying to discipline her but rather to help her challenge herself. Over e-mail it might have sounded like I was displeased with her work rather than concerned. It also made Sarah feel supported to have the three of us meet together to talk about the problem.

Understanding Independent School Parents

Classroom Visits

Another method of communication that should not be over-looked is observation. Invite parents into your classroom. Let them see what is really going on there. Invite them personally to school events. If they see that good things are going on they will be less likely to dwell on things they consider unsatisfactory. When I feel a parent is starting to be unhappy with the class, I invite them in as soon as possible to observe a lesson. They may not take me up on it but they realize that my door is wide open and I'm not trying to hide anything. If they do visit, they are likely to discover new ideas and be pleasantly surprised with what they find.

One year a student in my class left our school because "cheating was rampant in the second grade." Though the administration and I spoke at length with the family, they wouldn't change their minds and decided to leave. Understandably, this made other parents nervous. Luckily, I had lots of parents around helping that year and they knew the rumor wasn't true. When these parents were asked about what really was happening in the classroom, they were able to speak positively about the environment. The worried parents were able to separate one family's decision to leave from their own positive feelings about the school.

The Biggest Challenge: Managing Difficult Parents

Celebrate!

Since becoming a parent I have realized the power of celebration in an independent school classroom. It makes the parents feel good about the school their child is in and about this teacher in particular. If parents feel good about an event, they will be more likely to let go of some of the littler things that are bothering them. Bringing parents, teachers and students together in an upbeat atmosphere also gives a little more contact time between the parents and the teacher, allowing them the opportunity to get to know each other a little bit better, and each little bit helps teachers know better how to meet the parents' needs.

I have attended some terrific class celebrations. One year my son's pre-K class performed *The Wizard of Oz* complete with some original songs. The evening started with a potluck picnic on the lawn. The performance itself was outside. We all sat on the lawn together, eating a delicious meal, watching the sunset and listening to the children sing. It was a special night that I still remember in detail.

Another teacher I knew was studying astronomy with her class. She hosted a "full-moon night." Parents and children came late one evening to observe the night sky, drink hot chocolate and eat dessert. The teacher had invited a sidewalk astronomers group to set up telescopes on the roof of the school. The class got closer that night under the stars.

Understanding Independent School Parents

One year my class was studying parks. We set a goal of walking the length of Golden Gate Park (about five miles). We practiced with long walks around our campus. We studied maps of Golden Gate Park and chose sites we wanted to visit. We planned for some parents to meet us at a few points in case we couldn't do the whole walk. It took us most of the school day to walk the length of the park. We talked along the way and sang songs. When we got to Ocean Beach at the end the students ran towards the beach cheering. They were so proud of themselves! Not many parents were there with us that day but the feeling of accomplishment the students gained was immeasurable. When they went home and told their parents about it, you can be sure that the parents who weren't quite happy with the homework that week decided to let that go, as it now paled in comparison to the big event.

When my children participate in large events with their class, I often think, "My child is so lucky to be in *this* teacher's class. We are so lucky to be at this school. I am so glad that we have made the sacrifices necessary to send our children to this school." These feelings are important in a school where parents need to write a large check each year. They are also important in an environment where parent opinions carry a lot of weight.

Large classroom celebrations can take a lot of work. They require a teacher to come to school at a time outside the usual school day, which can be tiring after a whole day with students. Taking the time to create a special celebration, however, will pay large dividends.

The Biggest Challenge: Managing Difficult Parents

Parents will feel good about being in your class. This will be the event they talk about when they speak with other parents in the school. Administrators will celebrate your effectiveness with the parents and with others in the larger school community. You will connect with your class in a special way and when you get a difficult phone call or e-mail you will remember all the great experiences you have had with the class and keep the students in the front of your mind.

Chapter Seven

Face-to-Face: Surviving Parent Conferences

Pause for a minute. Tell yourself consciously that you are not going to have any parent conferences standing around in the library, on a field trip, or at the class play. Making that decision will save you, and the families you work with, much misunderstanding and grief. Parents *will* try and talk to you at these times — and of course you want to help them. But impromptu parent-teacher conferences are a bad idea. Nearly every time I have had an on-the-fly conference it has turned out poorly. My attention was not fully on the matter at hand and there were too many distractions for the parents to hear me and think about what I was saying.

If you have some difficult news to share, don't be tempted to do it on the fly in the hallway or on the sidelines of the soccer game. And don't wait until the regularly scheduled parent conference. Get in touch with the child's family and schedule a special meeting. "I noticed today that Sean was really having a hard time forming his letters, how can we work on this problem together?" Parents will appreciate you getting in touch with them when the incident occurs rather than waiting—and you will build trust with the family and show that you are working as part of a team. If you wait too long to tell them bad news it can feel as if you have been hiding something.

When a parent approaches you unexpectedly to discuss an issue say, "This matter is important to me and I would like to give it my full attention. Is there a time when we can meet to discuss it?" Practice saying this to yourself so that when a parent catches you in the hallway it will be on the tip of your tongue.

Now that you have set a time for a focused conference, read on:

- *Document, document, document.* Before you have a parent conference, there is a lot of work to be done. The first thing is to make sure that you have been documenting the student's academic and social progress throughout the year. Make sure the information is all dated and collected in one place (like your binder) so that you will have it at your fingertips during the conference.

- *Keep your administrator in the loop.* When things first start to get unusual with a family, make your administrator aware of the situation. This may be the only incident, but if more events occur the administration will be better able to support you. Having an administrator in your conference with a difficult parent is essential — and having an administrator who is fully apprised of the situation is even better. It is your administrator's job to make it possible for you to focus on teaching. If you are receiving five phone calls a day from the same family or an angry parent is always visiting your room, you need help. Administrators are more likely to help you if they do not get blindsided by information. Keep them informed and they will help you stay focused on the students.

- *Prepare an agenda.* Whether parents are coming in at your request or their own, or for their regularly scheduled conference, they should have a general idea of what to expect. If necessary, e-mail an agenda ahead of time to let them know what you want to discuss. If you have kept them apprised of what has been going on with their child all year this shouldn't be difficult. (Likewise, when a family receives a formal written report on their child, there should be no surprises in it!)

- *Follow the "Rule of Three."* Before the conference, sift through all your information and figure out which are the three most important ideas you want to convey. Yes, I know, sometimes they are 20 important ideas but you have to boil it down to three. It has been said that that is all people will remember! You can mention more things if you need to, but be sure you know your top three so that you can keep coming back to them and making sure they stick. You should wrap up the conference by touching on those three items one last time. If necessary, plan another meeting for a few weeks later and bring up three more main points.

- *Maintain "Talking Walls."* Let the walls do some of the work for you. Cover your classroom bulletin boards with work from your students. Make sure to put up an example from each child.

If you can, put some of the work outside the door where parents will be waiting. This could be a bulletin board or a table covered with stories the children have been writing. Parents will look at their child's work and look at some of the work the other children have been doing so that they can compare. They will get a sense of how their child is doing on their own and will be less surprised at what you have to say.

- *Dress for success.* Finally, dress the part. You are a professional and want to be perceived as one. Wear clothing that conveys this message. Parents will be more likely to think you know what you are talking about if you look professional. Often in the classroom we wear clothes that can get dirty, but for a conference you want to wear something a little nicer. When I'm working with the students, I wear khaki pants and a sweater to school. People laugh when they see me wearing a blazer. They know it must be a conference day!

At the Conference

Now that you have done all your preparations you are ready for your conference. Make sure to start on time. (There's no point in giving parents more fuel for their fire, right?). Stand up and shake the parents' hands as they enter your classroom or office. That's what people would do in a business meeting. It shows parents that you are a professional, too, and it says, "I want to make you comfortable here."

Next, let the parents know that you see their child as an individual. Share some special things you have noticed. Talk about an experience you have had with their child. Let the parents know that you are connecting with him or her as an individual as well as part of the group. Show them that you appreciate their child. This will help parents relax and trust you.

Once you have set the stage, you can share the hard news. Be direct and clear as you convey information. Avoid judgmental statements like, "Adam is sneaky." Instead, share what you have observed, "I have noticed that whenever we line up for recess Adam makes sure the teachers are not watching and then hits someone."

Make sure you have a plan to respond to any problems. Does the child need tutoring? Share evidence as to why you think so and then have the phone numbers of tutors available to hand to the parents. Does the child need a behavior contract? Have a rough draft available that you can look at together.

Let parents know that you want to work with them to make this a good year for their child. Keep mentioning that you want their child to be successful. This is what you are thinking, but parents need to hear you say it out loud.

A few minutes before the meeting ends ask the parents if they have any last questions. If there is still a lot to discuss, set another time for a follow-up meeting.

Reiterate what everyone is going to do next and then shake hands good-bye

A Successful Meeting

Mrs. Jackson had two sons, Andrew and David. Andrew was a child at another school when I met him. He needed to be challenged in math and so he came to me once a week to do different activities. Though Andrew didn't say much, he was quite a mathematician and enjoyed our weekly sessions. Each time after his lesson his mother and I would chat for a little bit about her son and about schooling in general. Through these weekly conversations she came to know me and trust me as a skilled educator.

Eventually Andrew came to our school and so did his brother, David. David was bright and quick like his brother but he had a few areas that needed shoring up. He needed occupational therapy to help him with his fine motor control; he had a hard time holding a pencil, even though he could do all the work. He also needed some social help, as he wasn't skilled at joining or working in groups.

The first year David was at our school, his teacher recommended tutoring assistance but the family decided not to pursue it. When David entered my class, it was clear that he still needed help and the longer we waited, the more difficult school was going to be for him. Mrs. Jackson and I already had a connection, so I decided to begin the conversations with just two of us rather than calling in an administrator. I had to figure out a way to help Mrs. Jackson see how helpful tutoring would be for David. Later, if my gentle approach wasn't working, I could call in an administrator for extra help.

During the second week of school, I called Mrs. Jackson and asked her to come in and talk with me about David. I shared some funny things that he had done during the first few days of school and then I asked, "What are your hopes and dreams for David for this year?" She shared that she knew he was having difficulty with his pencil grip and that sometimes he had a hard time in group situations.

I suggested that we get some outside OT help since that was area where David needed more practice than we could offer in the classroom. This area was also the most pressing because in the absence of legible handwriting it was hard to see evidence of what David had learned. I asked her if she had some techniques that she had found had worked to support David in group situations. I assured her we would try those techniques in the classroom to see how they went. We agreed to meet again the following month.

At our next meeting Mrs. Jackson told me that David had started OT. I told her I was so glad and could already see a difference in the classroom. Next I reported that we had tried the techniques she had suggested and had seen some improvement in David's group work. Then I shared some unusual situations by describing what I observed. I also told her that I thought some work with a professional might help David in group situations. Mrs. Jackson expressed her concern about the expense involved, and I sympathized. When parents are already paying so much for a private school education, it is hard to have extra expenses added on.

I suggested that Mrs. Jackson talk with a few other families who had been in similar situations and then we would meet again. After getting their permission, I gave Mrs. Jackson the names of a few families at our school and suggested that she call them. She did and agreed to go ahead with the extra help. By the end of the school year, David showed tremendous improvement in both areas. He felt good about his progress and his mom was proud of his work, as well.

I share this example to show how I slowly got a parent to support the idea of obtaining extra help for a child. Walking through the process step-by-step was crucial to gaining Mrs. Jackson's trust and giving her time to process the information. I started with one issue at a time and worked on it as a team with the family. Meeting frequently, starting with a meeting right at the beginning of the school year, helped me to build a strong relationship with them and showed that I was willing to do what was needed to help the child. At each meeting we considered if any adjustments needed to be made at school or at home.

Since this mother had come to know me through casual conversations earlier, she was willing to rely on my judgment and trust that I had the best interests of her child at heart. It so happened that the mother and I got to know each other before the school year began but we would also have had a chance to chat at the class play, her son's soccer game, or in the hallway at the end of the day. These conversations may seem inconsequential but they give you and the parent a chance to talk about a neutral topic and get to know each other. The more serious conversations that happen in a conference will go better for everyone as a result.

Weathering Conferences with the "5 Percenters"

Most parent conferences are places for conveying information. Conferences with 5 Percenters, however, are just to be gotten through. These conferences occur with parents with whom you have already communicated quite a bit without success. You know that you are not going to see eye-to-eye on any of the issues, yet you are required to offer them the opportunity for a conference. They, of course, can't wait to reopen the debate. Go into these conferences knowing that you have said your piece and have nothing new to say. You just have to get from one side of it to the other. Like most dentist appointments, it will be over in less than one hour.

One thing I do before a conference with a really difficult parent is invite an administrator or another teacher to join us. The ideal person is an administrator who has been following the family all along. If that person is not available, at least have another teacher with you. Having another person there helps everybody keep his or her behavior and comments in check. It also provides an observer you can talk to later to get their perspective.

Understanding Independent School Parents

A Conference Gone Wrong

One year, I faced a conference that I was dreading. I had repeatedly called the head of school and asked him to be present and he finally said that he would. The day of the conference came and the mother arrived right on time. I invited her and her son into the room. The head of school was not there yet but I expected him any minute, so I began. Big mistake! The mother began to yell at me and tell me how little her son had learned. She said it was the worst year her son had had at school. I couldn't believe what she was saying and I was stunned that she was saying it in front of her child.

Ten minutes later the head of our school arrived. The mother then turned on her charm and told him that I was the best teacher she had ever encountered. She praised all my efforts with her son and said he had made wonderful progress.

This was a parent with whom I was never going to be able to partner. She and I met many, many times over the course of the year. She had her own ideas about what her son's education should be and would not sway from them when discussing them with me — though she really changed her tune when the head arrived! Based on my previous experiences with her, I knew that it would not be possible to show her a different way of thinking at this conference. It was merely a meeting I had to get through. Since that was my goal, I needlessly put myself through the torture of the first 10 minutes of that meeting. I should have refused to start until the head of school arrived!

Face-to-Face: Surviving Parent Conferences

If you have to participate in a difficult conference, I have found it helpful to take notes. If the parents are upsetting you, just keep writing down what they're saying. They will feel that you are listening intently because they see that what they are saying is important enough for you to write down. And you will be glad you have these notes to refer to later on.

After a difficult conference, it is helpful to write a follow-up letter to the family restating your points. Keep a copy for yourself and also put one in the student's file. It is all right if the family does not agree with you. You have done your job by documenting your points.

Now here is a news flash for many teachers: If the conference gets really bad, you can leave! You do not have to stay in a hostile meeting. You can say quietly, "I'm sorry, this meeting has ceased to be productive. I think we should stop and continue at another time." I have sat through many conferences with parents yelling, crying, or screaming. I believed that it was my job to help parents see things from a different perspective so I sat there trying to explain myself again and again. It wasn't until years into my teaching career that someone pointed out that I had the right to be treated with respect and didn't have to endure abusive conferences. They also pointed out that if I were alone in a conference that went wrong I could ask the family to reschedule at another time when I could have another faculty member present.

Understanding Independent School Parents

A Painful Meeting

One year I had a first grader who used to sit in a corner by himself all day. He would just stare at his shoes. He rarely spoke to anyone and seldom did any work. At the beginning of first grade he did not know the letters of the alphabet so we began to work on those. I realized quickly that I wanted to have this student tested by a learning specialist but his parents objected. After a few failed attempts, I asked both parents to come to a meeting at school, and I asked my supervisor to attend. At the meeting I planned to show work samples from the boy and some of the other students. I hoped to convince his parents that some testing would help us figure out what to do and help us be more successful with their son. We had scheduled the meeting to last half an hour.

The parents arrived and they brought the boy's maternal grandmother with them. During the meeting the grandmother told me that in Finland they don't teach reading until children are nine years old. She felt it was not out of the ordinary for her grandson to not know his letters by the middle of first grade. Then the mother began to cry and told us how she didn't learn to read until third grade and her teachers called her stupid. Then the father began to cry and said if I only cared enough, his son would learn to read. He said he couldn't read until second grade when his teacher loved him and cared enough to teach him how to read. He escalated into yelling, telling me how unsympathetic I was.

Face-to-Face: Surviving Parent Conferences

As I listened, I kept hoping my administrator would bail me out of this mess, but he sat silently. The father stood up and stormed around the room yelling and crying. The grandmother started crying and murmuring in her native language. The mother wept on her mother's shoulder. After an hour and a half we were able to get the parents to agree to meet again at a later date since it seemed that we wouldn't make any progress that day. As we left the conference, I was shaking so much that I held onto my administrator's coat to steady myself as we left the room. I continued to shake for hours afterwards.

When thinking about all this later on, I realized that the parents had previous personal experiences that they were bringing into the conference. They were unable to see this situation clearly because their thinking was clouded by other information. This conference was not about the fact that I was a teacher who didn't "love their son enough." They were frustrated and distraught that their son was having the same difficulty learning to read that they had had themselves.

It never occurred to me that I could leave that conference. I did not realize that I had the power to say that it was unproductive and emotionally unsafe and that we would need to continue at another time. Perhaps I wasn't even thinking about that because there was an administrator there and I had trusted that he would handle the situation. Now I know that stopping a conference is an option if emotions get too high for the meeting to be productive.

Stopping an unproductive conference is one useful technique. I learned another from the head of our school. One year I was talking with her about another difficult conference that we were about to enter. She said, "Alison, figure out what you can give them."

This statement struck me as odd and actually made me angry. I was so frustrated with this family that I didn't want to "give" them anything. However, I realized what she was asking. By offering the family something, I could take some of the tension out of the meeting and help the parents calm down. What could I offer? An afternoon of tutoring, extra PE time, work with a mentor? My head was saying that I needed to figure out what was at the root of their concerns and offer something that might make them happier. The point of the conversation was to calm the parents, not to explain my philosophy. That could be a later conversation.

I have also found it helpful to hold difficult conferences somewhere other than my classroom. The first few conferences *should* be held in the classroom so that parents can get the idea of what a lively, engaging place it is. But sometimes it is necessary to hold the conference in a place that says, "We are taking you seriously." This could be a conference room or an administrator's office. By choosing another location you are letting parents know that this meeting is unusual and serious.

Face-to-Face: Surviving Parent Conferences

Communication Style

I want to close this chapter by mentioning the topic of language. If you have been in schools long enough, you realize that there is a specialized language that teachers use when working with families. Sam is not "lazy" he is just "not working up to his potential." Beth is not "weepy" she "has difficulty with transitions." Teachers who write narrative reports rather than report cards are especially skilled in using this other language, this "teacherese."

When a colleague heard I was working on this book she said, "Tell teachers they have to be direct. That is the best." But I am really torn on this issue because I know that sometimes that I have been direct and have really upset parents. At other times I have used "teacherese" and that hasn't been direct enough. For me this remains a tricky issue.

Right now, I feel that we teachers need to figure out each family's style and how they want (and are able) to hear information. And that is a tall order. We don't get to spend hours and hours getting to know parents. I almost want to give parents a checklist at the beginning of the year and have them check off whether they want the direct, semi-direct, or very gentle version of difficult information. That way we could be sure to give them what they needed all year!

Chapter Eight

Taking Care of Yourself: Strategies for Survival

As teachers we aspire to reach all of our students. In fact, we are asked to reach all of our students by accommodating their differences. We then try and do the same with the parents of our students. We strive to help them learn and we strive to build connections with them. This works most of the time. When it doesn't, it feels like as much of a failure as if one of our students didn't learn to subtract or cried every day when they had to come to school.

It is very hard to accept that we will not reach every parent. But we won't. Parents come into the classroom with other experiences that may be in the way of a productive parent-teacher relationship. Sometimes these hidden reasons cannot be overcome. In addition, we are working with people's most precious possessions, their children. Because of this, emotions are high — sometimes just too high to be productive.

It is okay if you sometimes have to let go of a few parents and keep the focus on the children. Some parents will push you to this point. Some parents will show you that they are not interested in working as part of a team. Some parents cannot be satisfied — ever. Do everything you can for the child in your classroom and accept that that is the best you can do. And take care of yourself!

Understanding Independent School Parents

Something that has helped me take care of myself through the years has been keeping a "thank you" binder. It is filled with pages and pages of thank-you notes and letters — and lately e-mails — from parents and students. All the little pictures and complimentary messages I receive during the year go into this binder. When the going gets tough, I pull it out. I look at the pictures from the children and remember how that many of them I have reached. Lots of children have been touched by my teaching and many appreciative parents have passed through my class.

Once, after a particularly difficult year with a parent, I was attending a seminar where I was invited to role-play the most difficult parent I'd ever had. My group designed a whole skit around this person and performed it in front of the other participants. I played the parent to the hilt — and it worked! The laughter from the audience helped me to laugh, too, and let go of my anger and frustration.

Another thing that has helped has been getting together with other colleagues from my school and sharing our stories. Try it. It helps to realize that you are not alone.

You've heard before that exercise reduces stress. Well, you can thank difficult parents for giving you extra motivation to exercise. With each step on the pavement you can pound out some of your aggression. I have swum my hardest and my fastest after a maddening meeting with a parent. All of this exercise will also help you sleep better — which is a good thing when you are tempted to lie awake all night thinking up witty retorts.

Taking Care of Yourself: Strategies for Survival

And when all else fails, you can write a book about your experiences!

Before I began this book, I wrote an open letter to parents one night in frustration. I felt that some of them needed tips on how to interact with teachers. I hoped that it could be published somewhere so parents could see it before the start of school. So here goes:

Dear Parents,

Greetings! Welcome back to a new school year! You must be full of excitement and expectation for your child. I too can feel the energy in the air as we set up the classroom, put names on all the folders, label the materials, open packages of new pencils, and decorate new bulletin boards.

Your child will need a homework folder, a backpack, and a lunchbox to prepare for the first day. But I wanted to offer you some tools that will help you prepare for the year ahead, as well.

There are some basic things that you can do to help your child be ready to learn each school day. Make sure that your child eats dinner, gets a good night's sleep, has breakfast, and has a healthy lunch. These may seem like "no-brainers," but you would be surprised how many children are not prepared in this way. I spend most of my one-on-one time with some children talking about how much sleep they have had or how hungry they are. I'm sure you would rather have me spend the time teaching your child instead.

You and I will become a team this year. As part of a team, it would be helpful if you would let me know when your child will be absent or if there are special circumstances when your child will need to leave early for an appointment. It is also very important for you to let me know if big events have happened in your child's life—such as a move, a divorce, or a death in the family. These events affect your child's state of mind. I cannot effectively guide your child's learning if I don't know that much of their energy is on other topics.

My goal and focus is to support your child. I want your child to be successful. That is my wish for the year. Every lesson I teach and interaction I have is with this end in mind. Please understand that I am working from my heart. If we do have a disagreement, please remember that, though you may disagree, I was doing what I thought was best for your child.

If difficulties do arise, please make an appointment to talk with me. It is very difficult for me to listen carefully to your concerns when you catch me in the hallway and I have children swarming around my legs.

Keep in touch with our classroom. Though you may not be able to be here each day, talk with your child about the topic we are studying, go with your child to the library and check out a book that is related to the topic, stop by the classroom once in a while and have your child show you around, or do something over the weekend that relates to what your child is learning.

I know your child is precious to you. I will do all I can to make your child feel valued, respected, safe, and challenged in our classroom. I am excited about this year of learning. Let the journey begin...
Sincerely,
Your child's teacher

Taking Care of Yourself: Strategies for Survival

I haven't shown this document to parents — until now — but writing it did make me feel better. So let us close this book with my letter. And let us remember that all of us — students and parents, teachers and administrators — are in this together.

About the Authors

Michael G. Thompson, a psychologist and school consultant, has worked with more than 500 schools in the U.S. and abroad. He is the author or co-author of nine books, including *Raising Cain: Protecting the Emotional Life of Boys*, and *Best Friends, Worst Enemies: Understanding the Social Lives of Children*. His newest book, *Homesick and Happy*, about summer camp, will be published by Ballantine Books in May 2012.

Alison Fox Mazzola has been a teacher in independent schools for over two decades. She is a co-owner of Building Understanding Math Workshops and currently leads workshops for parents, students, and teachers to help them improve their facility with math. She lives in Northern California with her husband and two children.

Made in the USA
Middletown, DE
17 August 2017